I0425574

DEDICATION

I dedicate this book first and foremost to my father, John M Cole, Sr., who always encouraged and supported me. My father, who was a World War II and Korean War veteran, always taught me to stand up and fight for what is right and always to respect and treat others as you would want them to treat you. My father never talked about his experiences during the war, but after his death, several veterans told me of how they owed their lives to my father's bravery during the war. He was a man of strong values, who loved his family and life in general. My father is a true hero and patriot who loved and fought for our great country and its freedoms. He will always be in my heart, and I miss him.

To my mother Yvette Cole, with her strong faith, positive attitude toward life, strong family values, who always sees the good in everyone and has always been there for those in need. She lived through the hell of the Nazi occupation of Alsace, France during WWII, and survived while seeing most of her close friends and family killed by the Nazi's. Her wisdom, positive attitude, strong Catholic faith and love for life is an inspiration to all who know her. Thank you, mom, for all your support and love!

To my children Jonathan, Kathryn, Abigail and Joseph who I love with all my heart, I want to thank them for their love and support in writing this book. They have brought great joy to my life and have helped me through some of the toughest times in my life.

And finally, to my wife Catherine, a hard working lady who always puts others before herself and who continues to support me on everything I do. She has been a big part of my life and a big inspiration for writing this book.

CONTENTS

ACKNOWLEDGEMENTS

I want to thank my brother and his wife, Gerald and Kelli Cole, for sharing their experiences and thoughts which assisted me in writing this book. I also would like to thank all the hard working Americans I have met throughout my travels across this great country and through my government service. Thank you all for sharing your experiences, thoughts and opinions which assisted in completing this book.

A special Thanks to John Kelly for his freindship and support in writing this book. John's stories of his life and adventures have been an inspiration and education.

Introduction

In 2016, Donald Trump was elected the 45th president of the United States. He won the Electoral College vote but not the popular vote receiving 304 Electoral College votes. His opponent, Hillary Clinton received 227 Electoral College votes. However, Donald Trump only received 46.1% of the popular vote compared to Hillary Clinton who received 48.2 %. Even though Donald Trump claims to have won the electoral college vote by a landslide and the popular vote his claims lack merit and fact.

Trump's presidential victory took many Americans and the world by surprise. After all, under President Obama, the economy was rebounding. We all should remember that toward the end of the George W. Bush presidency our country was heading for a depression. President Obama was able to implement policies which kept the country from financial collapse. In fact, under President Obama:

1. The unemployment rate decreased from 10% when he took office to 4.8%.
2. American workers began seeing an increase in wages.
3. The poverty rate in the U.S. declined
4. More Americans received health care benefits under the Affordable Care Act.
5. Laws and regulations were put in place to protect consumers and prevent another financial meltdown.

Despite accomplishments of President Obama's administration and the Democrats, Donald Trump, an individual who had never run for any political office surprisingly won the election. There are many theories on how Donald Trump was elected:

1. Many Americans tired of politicians wanted someone who was not a career politician: Donald Trump, a wealthy

businessman who campaigned on "draining the swamp", placing the best and brightest in his administration.

2. The Affordable Care Act - Trump campaigned on replacing the Affordable Care Act with a health care system that is more efficient and good for all Americans.
3. Trump campaigned on America to repair America's broken and outdated infrastructure. With very little money allocated over the years on repairing the infrastructure within the country, many Americans looked at this as a positive step to improving our country.
4. Americans didn't want Hillary Clinton as president.

Now that President Trump has been in office for close to two years Americans are beginning to see the impact he has made to the country and the world. So far President Trump has:

- passed a tax reform bill, the Tax Cut and Jobs Act, which provides tax cuts for corporations and wealthy Americans. He claims the bill benefits the middle and lower class and creates jobs, but that appears to be another lie. The tax reform bill has done very little in tax relief for the middle and lower income taxpayers and has not created any new jobs.
- Lied more than any president.
- Had more investigations against him than any sitting president
- Caused more social and economic division within the country
- Increased the national debt by 2 trillion dollars. His tax reform is the main reason for the increase. It should be noted that during his campaign he claimed he would decrease and eliminate the national debt.
- Increased our budget deficit by 319 billion dollars

- Put the U.S. in a trade war with our trade partners. His trade war has already hurt the U.S. economy. Due to the trade wars, taxpayers had to pay 12 billion dollars in aid to farmers for their losses.
- Made friends with dictators such as the Russian and North Korean leaders while putting down our Allies and leaders of the free world.

President Trump proposes a $4.75 trillion budget for the fiscal year 2020. He proposes to increase defence spending 5 per cent and slashing $845 billion from Medicare, $1.5 trillion in Medicaid, $25 billion in Social Security, $220 billion in Supplemental Nutrition Assistance Program (food stamps), $21 billion cut to Temporary Assistance for Needy Families, and $207 billion cuts in the Student loan program. All these cuts if passed will significantly impact the poor in our country and increase poverty and the working class. These proposed cuts go against the promises he made during his campaign not to cut Social Security and Medicare.

During his presidential campaign Trump, like most politicians made numerous promises and like many politicians, he accomplished or came close to accomplishing some of them. In that respect, he deserves credit. However, it will take time to determine if some of his policies will be beneficial to the country or divide it even further.

In regards to his slogan of making "America Great Again", America has always been a great country. Our country, like many countries in the world, has gone through tough times, but we as Americans seem to always come through making our country stronger. For year's people around the world looked up to our country as a place of opportunity, freedom and strength. Unfortunately, Trump has changed how the rest of the world looks at the U.S. through his isolationist policies, undiplomatic approach to foreign policy and threats.

What the Trump Administration Accomplished

To his credit, President Trump has been able to pass, with the assistance of a Republican majority in the Senate and House, a tax bill which lowers the corporate tax rate and taxes for the wealthy. The idea of lowering corporate taxes it that it would boost corporate profits and provide incentives to companies to stay in the U.S., hire more employees, and boost employee wages. Unfortunately, this idea which is similar to President Reagan's idea of trickle-down economics hasn't worked. Businesses are using the savings to boost corporate earnings and better pay for their executives, not the average worker. In fact, over the years companies have decreased worker's benefits to increase their profits. With fewer and fewer unions to protect workers, workers no longer have an advocate to fight for them.

The Economy

President Trump continues to boast about the U.S. economy claiming he is responsible for the low unemployment and rising stock market. It is possible his economic policies may have helped the economy. However, policy changes typically take years not months before showing their impact. That said, it will be a couple of years before his economic policies will reveal any significant changes, good or bad. For now, policies implemented by former President Barack Obama are what continues to thrive in the U.S. economy.

Americans seem to forget how the economy almost collapsed during George W. Bush's presidency. Policies implemented during his tenure were instrumental in causing the 2008 Great Recession which led to some of the highest unemployment and home foreclosures recorded in the U.S. since the Great Depression.

When President Barack Obama was elected president, he inherited the worst financial crises the U.S. has seen since the Great Depression.

- The U.S. unemployment rate peaked at 10 per cent in October 2009. [i]
- Real GDB fell roughly 4.3 per cent[ii]
- During the first quarter of 2009—the lowest point of the Recession—over 230,000 U.S. businesses closed.[iii]
- From 2007 to 2012, more than 450 banks failed across the country. [iv]
- Between 2006 and 2014, over 16 million homes foreclosed in the U.S., with nearly 3 million foreclosures each year at the peak of the crisis in 2009 and 2010. [v]

To President Obama's credit, he was able to turn the U.S. economy around. After leaving office after eight years, President Obama was able to:

- Reduce the unemployment rate from 10% to 4.8%; it continued to decrease after leaving office. [vi]
- Home prices increased by 20%[vii]
- Corporate profits increased by 57%[viii]
- 15.2 million more Americans received health insurance [ix]
- Illegal immigration dropped[x]

President Obama also implemented policies such as the Dodd-Frank Wall Street Reform and Consumer Protection Act to protect the economy and Americans by regulating unfair and predatory business practices.

Removed Policies Implemented by Former Administrations

Since being elected President, Donald Trump has removed most of the policies of Barack Obama and other Presidents to include:

- the Dodd-Frank Wall Street Reform and Protection Act - removing regulations which provided necessary government oversight on the financial institutions

- Reduced the operations of the Consumer Financial Protection Bureau which was implemented to assist consumers against unfair, deceptive and fraudulent business practices.
- Parts of the Affordable Care Act - reducing affordable health care to many Americans and increasing the poverty level in the United States.
- Ended a rule which allowed consumers to file class-action suits against financial companies.
- Repealed a bill mandating employers maintain records of workplace injuries
- Removing Environmental protection regulations –
    - Rejected bans on chemicals which have been known to cause harm to humans and animals
    - Rolled back emissions rules allowing companies to produce higher toxic emissions in the atmosphere.
    - Repealed the Waters of the United States rule
    - Ending the ban prohibiting dumping waste from mining into streams.
    - Allow the drilling for oil in the Arctic
    - Withdrew rules on regulating fracking on public land.
- Withdrew from the Trans-Pacific Partnership
- Withdrew the U.S. from the Paris Climate Accord
- Reversed a ban on civil forfeiture
- The repealed rule mandating Internet service providers seek permission before selling personal information
- Cancelled public reporting on visitors to the White House

Raised the Deficit and Debt

Although President Trump pledged he would reduce the deficit and spending, his policies have increased the deficit. In the fiscal year 2018, the deficit rose to $779 billion, up 17% from the previous year, according to the Treasury Department. That's the largest number since 2012 when the country was still spending massively to stimulate an economy struggling to recover.
Due to the Republican-backed tax cuts, corporate tax collections fell $76 billion or 22% while government spending increased. [xi]

The last time the U.S had no deficit was during President Bill Clinton's presidency. From 1998 – 2001 the U.S. had a surplus. In 2002 under George W. Bush the U.S. went from a surplus to a deficit partially due in part from government spending after the September 11th attacks, the U.S. wars in Afghanistan and Iraq and policy changes. Under Presidents George W. Bush and Barack Obama, the U.S. deficit continually increased leaving the U.S. 6.785 trillion dollars in debt.

In 2018 the deficit rose 17% under President Trump increasing the U.S. national debt. According to Government Budget Office, the U.S. debt is projected to climb even higher under President Trump with no relief in sight. In fact, according to the U.S. Treasury Department as of January 3, 2019, the U.S. debt is 21.94 trillion.

Has the Record for Making False and Misleading Statements

There is no doubt most politicians' skew facts and statistics to enhance their arguments on certain positions. However, according to the Washington Post, President Trump has made 8158 false claims or misleading statements in the two years of his presidency, more than any other president.[xii]

Trump Leads the Number of Investigations on a sitting U.S. President

Presently, there are numerous investigations on President Trump and individuals he selected and placed in his administration. They include investigations on Russia's meddling in U.S. elections, obstruction of justice, illegal campaign finance activities, and other illegal activity.

The Special Counsel Investigation, also known as the Mueller investigation, began in May 2017 to look into Russian interference in the 2016 elections. In June 2017, it was expanded to include looking into possible obstruction of justice charges by Trump and his administration.

Since its inception, the investigation has resulted in criminal charges against over 30 individuals and three Russian entities. The individuals charged with crimes include some President Trumps closest associates and members of his staff. They include:

Michael Cohen – Trump's lawyer and personal fixer. Mr Cohen worked for Mr Trump for over 12 years. In August 2018, he pled guilty to five counts of tax evasion, one count of falsifying submissions to a bank and two counts of campaign finance violations. The counts of campaign finance violations have to do with Mr Cohen arranging payments to Karen McDougal and Stephanie Clifford for their silence on their alleged affairs with Mr Trump.

Mr Cohen told a federal judge he made the payments under the direction of Mr Trump to influence the election. Mr Trump initially denied knowing the two women or the payments which were made but later acknowledged he reimbursed Mr Cohen $130,000 for the payments.

Paul Manafort – Trump's former campaign chairman. In September 2018 he pled guilty to conspiracy against the United States and conspiracy to obstruct justice. Mr Manafort agreed to cooperate with the Mueller investigation but breached the plea agreement by lying to the FBI and Special Counsel's office.

In an earlier case which stemmed from the Special Counsel's office, Manafort was found guilty on eight of eighteen counts on tax and bank fraud stemming from failing to pay taxes on millions of dollars pro-Russian politicians in Ukraine paid him.

Rick Gates, a top aide and deputy campaign chairman to Mr Trump pled guilty to financial fraud and lying to federal investigators in Feb. 2018. Mr Gates testified that he and Manafort used offshore bank accounts and wire transfers to hide money paid by pro-Russian politicians in Ukraine from the IRS.

Michael Flynn, Mr Trump's first national security advisor. In Dec. 2017 he pled guilty to lying to the FBI about his contacts with the Russian ambassador, Sergey Kislyak. As part of a plea agreement, he agreed to cooperate with the Special Counsel's office.

George Papadopoulos, a junior foreign policy advisor to the Trump campaign who pled guilty to lying to the FBI, lied about his interactions with a London professor with links to the Russian government. The professor told Papadopoulos that the Russians had thousands of emails which contained "dirt" on Hillary Clinton. He used his connections to arrange a meeting with members of the Trump campaign and the Russians.

W. Samuel Patten pled guilty in Aug. 2018 to failing to register as a foreign agent. He allegedly partnered with a Russian national to lobby on behalf of the pro-Russian party in Ukraine. He received over a million dollars for his work which included setting up meetings with members of Congress and government officials. His case was referred to the U.S. Attorney's office by the Special Counsel's office.

Roger Stone, a longtime informal advisor to President Trump. Mr Stone was charged with seven counts including witness tampering, making false statements about Russian interference in the 2016 elections and obstruction of justice. The Special Counsel's office claims Mr Stone was in regular contact with WikiLeaks and the

Trump campaign during the release of stolen emails from the Democratic National Committee and Clinton campaign. According to the indictment, a senior Trump campaign official was directed to contact Mr Stone about additional damaging information Wikileaks had regarding the Clinton campaign.

Twelve Russian Intelligence Officers were indicted on numerous charges to include hacking of the Democratic National Committee and Hillary Clinton campaign email accounts and servers.

the Konstantin Kilimnick, a Russian national charged with obstruction of justice attempted to persuade witnesses to lie to a jury in the case against Mr Manafort.

Investigations by the US Attorney for the Southern District of New York

There are several investigations n the US Attorney for the southern district of New York on the financial transactions of the Trump Organization, the Trump inauguration committee, Trump SuperPact funding, and foreign lobbying.

Investigations by New York City and New York State

New York State and City are investigating Trump's tax payments.

Despite Trump's denial of any Russian collusion most of his aids and family members have had numerous contacts with known Russian intelligence agents which the Mueller investigation has already uncovered. The question remains did Donald Trump aware of Russian involvement. He continues to lie and mislead the American public so we will have to wait and see what the Mueller investigation uncovers and rely on the facts.

Life in the United States under Trump's Presidency

Since the election of Donald Trump as president of the United States Americans have seen a greater division both economically and ethnically in our county. There is also a greater uncertainty on the future of our country with Trump's trade wars, immigration, foreign and economic policies, and continuous lying to the American public. Not one of President Trump's policies has assisted the poor or middle class in our country. They have only helped his businesses and the upper class. Unlike any other president, he has alienated most of our allies and supported most of the worst dictators in the world such as President Putin in Russia and Kim Jung-Un of North Korea. Many of our allies are moving away from the U.S. dependence and are looking at economic and defence alternatives which will dramatically reduce U.S. world influence and could financially hurt the U.S. financially.

As previously stated, the U.S.ecomomy began to improve under President Obama and was flourishing when Trump became president. However, the policies he has implemented since he was elected have caused the economy to slow down and the deficit to increase.

Trump's Tax cuts and Jobs Act did very little for the middle and lower income Americans while greatly benefiting upper-income Americans and businesses. It has also caused our deficit to increase due to lower tax revenue.

On 4 May 2018, the United Nations Human Rights Council in a report titled "Report of the Special Rapporteur on extreme poverty and human rights on his mission to the United States of America" reported in its overview the following in regards to the United States.

About 40 million live in poverty, 18.5 million in extreme poverty, and 5.3 million live in Third World conditions of absolute poverty. It has the highest youth poverty rate in the Organization for Economic Cooperation and Development (OECD), and the highest infant mortality rates among the comparable OECD States. Its citizens live shorter and sicker lives compared to those living in all other rich democracies, eradicable tropical diseases are increasingly prevalent, and it has the world's highest incarceration rate, one of the lowest levels of voter registrations in among OECD countries and the highest obesity levels in the developed world. [xiii]

The United States has the highest rate of income inequality among Western countries. The $1.5 trillion in tax cuts in December 2017 overwhelmingly benefited the wealthy and worsened inequality. The consequences of neglecting poverty and promoting inequality are clear. The United States has one of the highest poverty and inequality levels among the OECD countries, and the Stanford Center on Inequality and Poverty ranks it 18th out of 21 wealthy countries regarding labour markets, poverty rates, safety nets, wealth inequality and economic mobility. But in 2018 the United States had over 25 per cent of the world's 2,208 billionaires.6 There is thus a dramatic contrast between the immense wealth of the few and the squalor and deprivation in which vast numbers of Americans exist. For almost five decades the overall policy response has been neglectful at best, but the policies pursued over the past year seem deliberately designed to remove basic protections from the poorest, punish those who are not in employment and make even basic health care into a privilege to be earned rather than a right of citizenship. The visit of the Special Rapporteur coincided with the dramatic change of direction in relevant United States policies. [xiv]

The new policies:

(a) provide unprecedentedly high tax breaks and financial windfalls to the very wealthy and the largest corporations;

(b) pay for these partly by reducing welfare benefits for the poor;
(c) undertake a radical programme of financial, environmental, health and safety deregulation that eliminates protections mainly benefiting the middle classes and the poor;

(d) seek to add over 20 million poor and middle-class persons to the ranks of those without health insurance;

(e) restrict eligibility for many welfare benefits while increasing the obstacles required to be overcome by those eligible;

(f) dramatically increase spending on defence, while rejecting requested improvements in key veterans' benefits;

(g) do not provide adequate additional funding to address an opioid crisis that is decimating parts of the country; and

(h) Make no effort to tackle the structural racism that keeps a large percentage of non-Whites in poverty and near poverty.[xv]

In a 2017 report, the International Monetary Fund (IMF) captured the situation even before the impact of these aggressively regressive redistributive policies had been felt stating that the United States economy "is delivering better living standards for only the few", and that "household incomes are stagnating for a large share of the population, job opportunities are deteriorating, prospects for upward mobility are waning, and economic gains are increasingly accruing to those that are already wealthy". The share of the top 1 per cent of the population in the United States has grown steadily in recent years. In 2016 they owned 38.6 per cent of total wealth. Concerning both wealth and income, the share of the bottom 90 per cent has fallen in most of the past 25 years. The tax reform will worsen this situation and ensure that the United States remains the most economically divided society in the developed world. The planned dramatic cuts in welfare will essentially shred crucial dimensions of a safety net that is already full of holes. Since economic and political power reinforces one another, the political system will be even more vulnerable to capture by wealthy elites.[xvi]

This situation bodes ill not only for the poor and middle class in America but for society as a whole, with high poverty levels "creating disparities in the education system, hampering human capital formation and eating into future productivity." There are also global consequences. The tax cuts will fuel a global race to the bottom, thus further reducing the revenues needed by Governments to ensure basic social protection and meet their human rights obligations. And the United States remains a model whose policies other countries seek to emulate. Defenders of the status quo point to the United States as the land of opportunity and the place where the American dream can come true because the poorest can aspire to the ranks of the richest. But today's reality is very different. *The United States now has one of the lowest rates of intergenerational social mobility of any of the rich countries.* Zip codes, which are usually reliable proxies for race and wealth, are tragically reliable predictors of a child's future employment and income prospects. High child and youth poverty rates perpetuate the intergenerational transmission of poverty very effectively and ensure that the American dream is rapidly becoming the American illusion.

The equality of opportunity, which is so prized in theory, is in practice a myth, especially for minorities and women, but also for many middle-class White workers. New technologies now play a central role in either exacerbating or reducing poverty levels in the United States. Some commentators are singularly optimistic in this regard and highlight the many potential benefits of new technologies, including those based on artificial intelligence, for poverty reduction efforts in fields as diverse as health care, transportation, the environment, criminal justice, and economic inclusion. Others acknowledge the downsides, and especially the potential negative effects of automation and robotization on future employment levels and job security. But remarkably little attention has been given to the specific impact of these new technologies on the lives of the poor in American society today. Such inquiries have significance well beyond that of the poor since experience shows that those in poverty are often a testing ground for practices and policies subsequently applied more broadly. In the present report, the Special Rapporteur seeks to stimulate deeper reflection on the impact of new technologies on the human rights of the poorest.[xvii]

The entire 20-page report digs deeper into the impact of Trump's policies and is something every American should read. It also helps describe what life is like for Americans under the Trump Administration. Shortly after the release of this report, President Trump withdrew the U.S. from the U.N. Human Rights Council. It is a common theme of Trump to withdraw or attack any person or agency that goes against him.

The lower and middle-class Americans continue to struggle to make ends meet despite the lower unemployment many having to work two or three jobs to meet their basic needs. According to the Department of Labor, half the jobs in America pay less than $18 an hour which is less than a living wage (living wage is the income necessary for an individual to meet basic needs). Also, over the past two decades, many companies have reduced or taken away benefits such as health care and retirement, to their employees leaving working Americans unable to afford health care and saving for retirement.

United States Decline - No Longer a World Leader

The United States used to be a country looked upon as the best place in the world to live. It was at one time considered a country of opportunity, freedom, and power. However, over the past few decades that perception has diminished and for many Americans, the American dream has become less and less a possibility.

According to the U.S. Census Bureau and UNICEF reports:

- 1 in 7 Americans, 46.5 million people, to include 20% of American children now live in poverty. In fact, since 2004, poverty rates in the U.S. have consistently exceeded those of other wealthy nations. The nation's official poverty rate in 2014 was 14.8 per cent, which means there were 46.7 million people in poverty.[xviii]

- There is a higher poverty rate in the US than in many other countries.[xix] The graph below is from the Economic Policy Institute report dated 24 July 2012. It shows the United States listed at the very bottom, with a higher poverty rate than most other democratic countries.

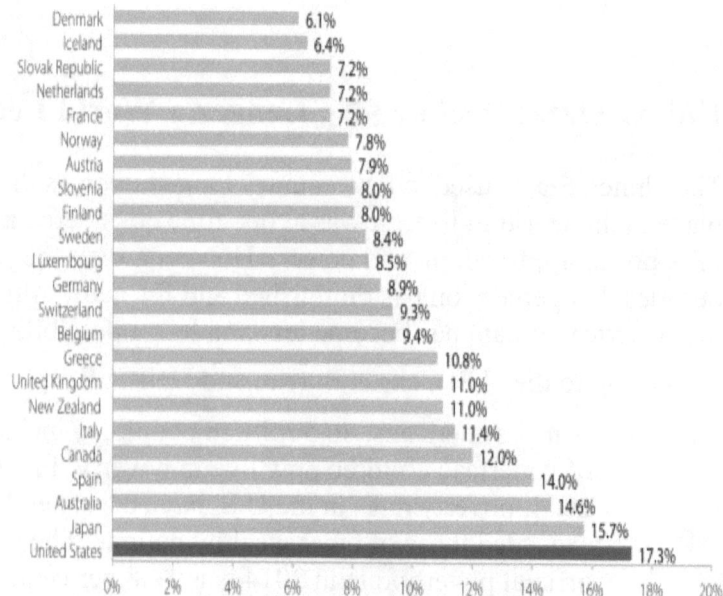

Country	Percentage
Denmark	6.1%
Iceland	6.4%
Slovak Republic	7.2%
Netherlands	7.2%
France	7.2%
Norway	7.8%
Austria	7.9%
Slovenia	8.0%
Finland	8.0%
Sweden	8.4%
Luxembourg	8.5%
Germany	8.9%
Switzerland	9.3%
Belgium	9.4%
Greece	10.8%
United Kingdom	11.0%
New Zealand	11.0%
Italy	11.4%
Canada	12.0%
Spain	14.0%
Australia	14.6%
Japan	15.7%
United States	17.3%

- In 2011, government reports showed that half the U.S. population qualified as low income.

- A report by the United Nations Children's Fund, on the well-being of children in 35 developed nations shows the United States ranks 34th out of 35 countries surveyed. More than one in five American children fall below a relative poverty line, which UNICEF defines as living in a household that earns less than half of the national median. [xx]

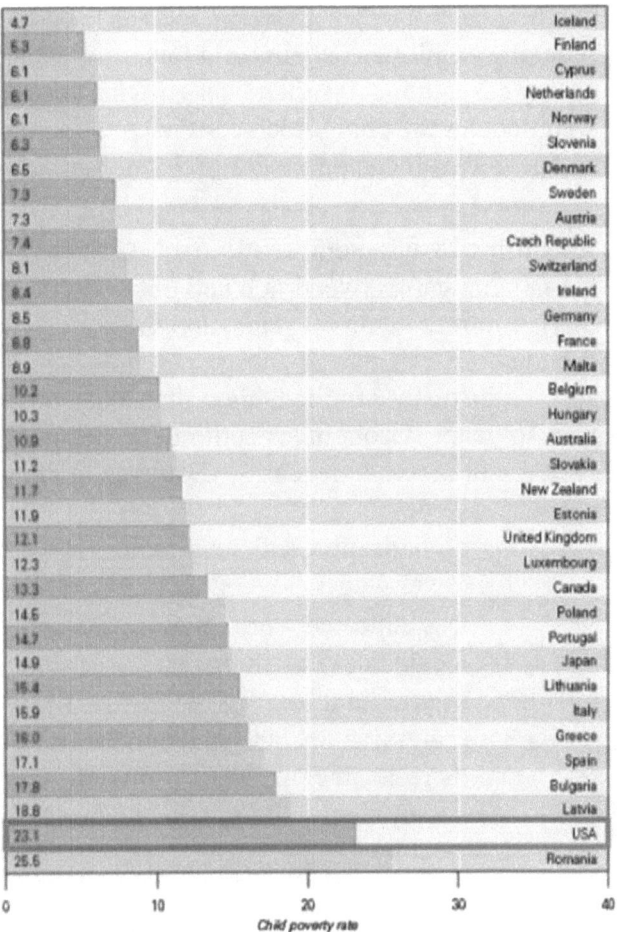

Value	Country
4.7	Iceland
6.3	Finland
6.1	Cyprus
6.1	Netherlands
6.1	Norway
6.3	Slovenia
6.5	Denmark
7.3	Sweden
7.3	Austria
7.4	Czech Republic
8.1	Switzerland
8.4	Ireland
8.5	Germany
8.8	France
8.9	Malta
10.2	Belgium
10.3	Hungary
10.9	Australia
11.2	Slovakia
11.7	New Zealand
11.9	Estonia
12.1	United Kingdom
12.3	Luxembourg
13.3	Canada
14.5	Poland
14.7	Portugal
14.9	Japan
15.4	Lithuania
15.9	Italy
16.0	Greece
17.1	Spain
17.8	Bulgaria
18.8	Latvia
23.1	USA
25.5	Romania

Child poverty rate

The above data and charts show how our country ranks among other countries in regards to poverty. It is disturbing that the United States has one of the highest ranking poverty levels among other advanced countries. As Americans, we should be spending more resources in correcting the poverty in our country, but unfortunately, many Americans appear to be oblivious to the plight of the poor in our country.

There are many different opinions on why the poverty level is so high in our country. Some want us to believe it's due to high unemployment, lack of education, or laziness while others see it as due to a lack of opportunity, an increase in greed with employers reducing employee benefits and lowering wages to increase profits. In any case, the fact is there is a growing inequality between the wealthy and the poor which continues to increase every year which I believe we all can agree is a problem that needs to be corrected.

According to a September 11, 2012, U.S. Census Bureau report, the income gap between rich and poor people grew to the widest margin in more than 40 years, and the poverty rate is at a two-decade high.[xxi]
Income inequality in the United States has been increasing over the past 40 years. Economists continue to debate the reasons for the increase in income inequality. Some economists believe it is partially due to:

- globalisation with companies relocating to areas with lower wages,
- less educated workers
- the decrease in unions which protected workers' rights, salaries and benefits
- regressive tax laws and anti-labour policies – due to the increase in conservative movements
- government policies which cater to big business and the wealthy

I believe all the above play a part in the increased division of wealth and causes of income inequality in our country, and all have a common theme - greed.

In 2012, an article in Forbes magazine highlighted the issue of income inequality within the United States and produced the below chart showing income inequality is very close to that in 1928 before the Great Depression. Since the article and under the Trump administration income inequality has further increased.

There are many theories on what caused the Great Depression, but most economists agree that it was due to lack of government oversight of the financial sector and the lack of government policy. One of the reasons government policy and regulations were established after the Great Depression to ensure it would not repeat itself.

Annual U.S. income share of the Top 1%

25%

1928: 23.9%

Great Depression

2007: 23.5%

20%

15%

10%

1980: 10%

5%

1910   1930   1950   1970   1990   2010 xxii

U.S. companies are only concerned about profit and very unsympathetic to the American workers who lost their jobs, their livelihood or the families they support. To save money some companies have moved parts of their manufacturing facilities to countries where labour is cheaper, and labour laws are nonexistent. They have done this to increase corporate profits.

Our elected officials continue to pass legislation which has led to the deregulation of labour markets, privatisation of some public functions and decreases in the top marginal tax rates. We as citizens have always been proud of the fact that our country is based upon principles of a truly democratic system and a government that is for the people and by the people. Unfortunately, that has not been the case for several decades; our country is no longer run by its citizens but by special interests groups that spend millions of dollars on promoting the candidate that best suits their needs and not that of our country.

Many companies have cut employee benefits to the bone to raise their profit margins leaving many employees and families with inadequate health insurance and little to no retirement benefits.

Working Americans continue to struggle to meet their basic needs finding it more and more
difficult to get ahead financially. We see it throughout our country average working Americans trying to provide for their families, many living from paycheck to paycheck. Many are unable to afford medical insurance and those who can still hope no unexpected events such as:

- A family member is having medical issues which can wipe out any savings they may have or putting them further in debt.
- Being laid off from their job or receiving a reduction in salary,
- Their car or furnace breaks causing them to fall further in debt and unable to provide basic needs for their family.

Companies have dehumanised employees treating them like machines or a number, not like individuals trying to support themselves and their families. Many companies have significantly reduced health insurance and retirement benefits for their employees as well and in some cases salary or wages to increase company profits and please shareholders.

According to the National Endowment for Financial Education (NEFE) a survey conducted by Harris Interactive found that from 2007 through 2012, 40% per cent of employed adults in the United States have seen their employee benefits packages decreased—or eliminated. And for seven in 10 of the employees who have experienced cutbacks, health insurance coverage has been the hardest hit, resulting in higher deductibles, higher co-pays, and costly premiums.[xxiii] The decrease in employee benefits appears to be a growing trend in our country which is getting worse every year. Employees shoulder more costs, including higher deductibles and co-pays, as well as more expensive premiums as employers cut back on benefits to increase profit. The cost of health insurance, retirement savings, and other benefits has increased for employees, thus substantially reducing the take-home pay they receive. For many, this reduction in pay leaves very little income for individuals to survive on. Since they are no longer paying for these benefits, companies see an increase in profits and employees see a decrease in salary.

What Caused Our Decline - Greed, Selfishness and loss of Christian Values?

In his Farewell Address of September 1796, George Washington stated "virtue or morality is a necessary spring of popular government,"[xxiv] while John Adams claimed that statesmen "may plan and speculate for Liberty, but it is Religion and Morality alone, which can establish the Principles upon which Freedom can securely stand."[xxv]

The founders of our country understood the importance of religion and our Christian beliefs when they wrote the Constitution, the foundation of what our country is based. Christianity still plays an enormous role in the politics of our country. The largest religion in the US is Christianity, claimed by the majority of the population (73% in 2012).

The middle class and poor American families struggle to provide the basic needs for their family, food, clothing, medical care, and shelter. As parents, we all want to see our children succeed in life. We not only want to provide them with the basic needs to help them grow and become productive adults but also want to see them have the opportunity to attend college or a trade school which will hopefully provide them with the necessary tools for a better life. Unfortunately, for most Americans, the ability to provide for their families has become more difficult over the years. Many have lost their jobs, and others have seen their salary and benefits cut or abolished.

Over the years, many workers have slowly seen their company benefits, such as retirement plans and health insurance, cut to reduce employee costs and increase company profits. The reduction of benefits are partially due to the reduction in unions which were established to be a voice for the worker and changes in government laws which protected workers such as the Multiemployer Pension Reform Act of 2014.

American workers, especially the middle class and poor, continue to struggle while the wealthy continue to fill their pockets off the profits made from hardworking Americans. Unfortunately, there are also a few individuals who are lazy, who refuse to work and expect the government and everyone else to support them. These lazy individuals add additional burden on those who work and pay taxes.

The decline in the United States can be attributed to many factors to include income inequality, the 2008 great recession, global economic decline, bad policy decisions over the years, and decline in the Christian values our country. An increase in greed and selfishness within our society also attributed to the economic division.

The belief of some Americans that the poor are lazy and don't matter was seen in the past presidential election when Mitt Romney was secretly taped commenting that "There is 47 per cent of the people who will vote for the president no matter what … who are dependent upon government, who believe that they are victims. … These are people who pay no income tax. … and so my job is not to worry about those people. I'll never convince them that they should take personal responsibility and care for their lives." Romney's comment reinforces the attitude and belief of some (primarily the wealthy) that the poor in this country don't matter because they don't take personal responsibility a belief that is far from the truth. Anyone who has had to work and struggle to care for their family knows how difficult it can be and at times it seems even impossible. Add unemployment and other unforeseen problems which are not under their control and the struggles become even more difficult.

What is also disturbing about Mitt Romney's comment is he professes to be a Christian; he is a member of the Church of Jesus Christ of Latter Day Saints, Mormon, religion. I want to believe the Mormon Church, as well as other Christian churches, teach Christian values which include the importance of helping the poor.

Americans as a whole are very compassionate, sympathetic and caring people. Most Americans want a fair common sense system of government. There has been so much deception and misinformation from both parties and special interest groups related to government and social issues; it is hard to understand what is true or factual and what is completely inaccurate. Most Americans are tired of politicians who were reflected in our last presidential election when Donald Trump, who ran on a platform that he was not a politician, was elected our president.

In a perfect world everyone would earn a living wage, pay their fair share of taxes, receive assistance only in desperate situations and only until they can get themselves back on their feet, business would make profits but also understand the needs of their employees and their communities. Since we don't live in a perfect world changes which are fair and equal to all are necessary with the proper amount of oversight to ensure changes continue to be fair.

The question remains will both parties ever get together to resolve their differences for the overall welfare of the country and its citizens or will they continue to fight each other on every issue, continue to succumb to special interest groups and wealthy donors thus jeopardising the best interest of the country.

The Great Recession

The Great Recession, which began under George W. Bush and continued under Barak Obama's presidency, should have been a wake-up call to all Americans. Like the Great Depression of the 1920s and 1930's the Great Recession was due in part with the deregulation of the banking and financial institutions and greed. In 1999 Congress passed the Gramm-Leach-Bliley Act (GLB), also known as the Financial Services Modernization Act of 1999 which allowed the consolidation of commercial banks, investment banks, financial and insurance companies. The bill enacted on 12 November 1999, which Republicans readily endorsed and President Bill Clinton signed into law was approved after millions of dollars in campaign contributions and soft money donations to Republicans and Democrats by investment banks and other financial services companies. The bill intended to allow financial institutions more flexibility to expand their operations thus becoming more competitive was supposed to assist consumers. However, instead, the bill assisted banks and financial institutions in monopolising the markets bringing them huge profits.

In the 2000s the real estate market boomed causing home prices to soar. Homeowners seeing the increased equity in their homes refinanced and used the money to live their "American dream" on credit not thinking the market would collapse and believing home prices would continue to rise. With the ease of regulations, financial institutions were able to make new loans or refinance existing loans with ease. In 2008 when the market began to slump into a global crisis, people began to panic. By September 2008, average U.S. housing prices had declined by over 20% from their mid-2006 peak.[xxvi][xxvii]

Deregulations of the financial institutions allowed access to credit to individuals who previously would not have been able to obtain a loan due to poor credit or low income. Individuals who overextended themselves found it easy to refinance their home loan using the equity in their home to pay off their credit card bills and loans. Many were encourages by financial institutions and chose to refinance using adjustable-rate mortgages which lower their initial monthly payments. These adjustable-rate mortgages enticed borrowers with an initial below-market interest rate which was affordable until the rates increased. Once the rates increased some individuals found they were unable to afford the higher monthly payments and seeing the equity in their homes decline, some lower than what they already owed on their home began to default. During 2007, there were nearly 1.3 million properties in foreclosure proceedings, a 75% increase over 2006.[xxviii] The foreclosures increased to 2.3 million in 2008, an 81% increase vs 2007.[xxix]

At the peak of the crisis, the government under President Barack Obama implemented emergency monetary and fiscal authorities to stabilise the global financial system which prevented a downward spiral which may have been a second Great Depression.

U.S. Policymakers, Republicans and Democrats, deserve a share of the blame for their inability or unwillingness to keep taps and proper oversight on the financial sector which put the U.S. in one of its deepest recession since the 1930s. As citizens, we are partially to blame for electing policymakers that allow special interests groups to control legislation.

Special Interest Groups

The Merriam-Webster dictionary defines special interests as "a person or group seeking to influence legislative or government policy to further often narrowly defined interests."

Special Interest groups, unfortunately, play a significant role in our election process and in formulating our government policies. Elections are no longer won by winning the support of the average American but winning the support of wealthy donors and special interest groups. Politicians from both the Republican and Democrat parties vote on and promote legislation which benefits the special interest groups that help fund their elections and not necessarily what is best for the country or its citizens. Our democracy and democratic values, therefore, have deteriorated due to the influence special interest group's levy on our political system and process. There are numerous special interest groups which play a significant role in influencing our political system. For example:

- The National Rifle Association (NRA) spends an enormous amount of money and resources to defeat any politician who tries to pass common sense gun laws.
- Big businesses push for fewer government regulations and taxes to increase profits
- Many religious organizations push laws which promote their beliefs such as anti-abortion laws
- Labour groups push for better benefits for workers as well as more power,

The increasing use of political action committees (PACs) is another form of special interest used to influence our country's politicians and our citizens. A PAC is a committee formed by an organization, industry, or individual to collect money and then contributing that money to selected political candidates and causes. PACs concentrate the financial clout of large numbers of individuals and can, therefore, influence public policy more effectively than can a single, ordinary individual.

While some states such as Maine and California limit the amount of money that PACs can contribute to state elections, in Texas these groups may give as much as they wish.

Religious organizations and groups promote candidates they feel will promote legislation which adheres to their religious beliefs, which would be good if these groups promoted candidates who support the overall beliefs of most religions which are helping the poor. Christianity promotes fairness, treating others as we would want to be treated and helping those who are in need – the poor.

> *Deuteronomy 15: There will always be poor people in the land. Therefore I command you to be openhanded toward your fellow Israelites who are poor and needy in your land.*

Unfortunately, there are Christian groups that promote candidates who don't believe in supporting the less fortunate but their agendas. As a Catholic, I was taught that we should always help the poor and needy. It shocks me that the church spends a lot of resources on promoting anti-abortion candidates instead of using those resources to help the less fortunate. I don't agree with abortion. However, I believe it is an individual's choice. God is the one who will judge each one of us on what we do in our lives. It is disturbing that the so-called Christians who want to end abortion are the same individuals who want the government to cut aid to the poor. They claim to be Christian but are hypocrites. Churches should be there to provide guidance and assistance to individuals who need help not condemn them. Jesus Christ was a radical in his day, and today he would be considered a socialist which probably offends a lot of people. Religious organizations should be in the business of teaching, saving souls and helping the less fortunate not politics.

All these groups spend enormous amounts of money to sell and promote their self-serving agendas. Most of which are not necessarily what is best for our country yet we as Americans seem to buy into their propaganda. Politicians refuse to pass legislation to control the influence of special interests groups place on our system because they rely on these groups to help them get elected.

They need the financial backing these groups can provide for their election campaigns and therefore sell their souls to these groups in return for their backing. As long as we allow special interests groups to influence government policy and our elected officials, we will continue to be slaves to them. As citizens, we need to demand limits on money and influence special interest groups have on our election process. Proper legislation can limit the influence of special interest groups. The legislation should include public disclosure requirements that provide transparency on what organizations and groups donate to what political candidate; and require politicians to provide full disclosure on all their campaign funding. Of course, if we only allowed politicians to use public financing to run their campaigns, it would take out the need for support from special interests groups.

Unfortunately, many Americans don't take an active role in our countries political system and have a very limited understanding of it and the individuals they elect. Many Americans tend to believe:
- Some of the political ads paid for by special interest groups many of which distort facts,
- Some vote for the candidate based on party,
- While others tend to vote for a candidate based solely on a single issue such as abortion.

As Americans and Christians, we need to begin taking a stronger stance on learning and understanding our political system and the officials we elect to take back the system of government. A system established for the people and by the people, not for just a few individuals who want to use the system to get rich.

If Americans elect individuals, who are sincere about doing what is best for our country maybe then we as Americans can push for changes which will benefit the country and its entire people.

Greed

Luke 12-15 - Then he said to them, "Watch out! Be on your guard against all kinds of greed; life does not consist in an abundance of possessions."

As individuals we all would love to make enough to support our families, have a decent place to live and raise our families, and maybe take our family on vacation once a year. Unfortunately, for many Americans, it is an impossible dream. According to U.S. Census Bureau's estimates for 2015, an estimated 43.1 million Americans, 13.5% of the population lives in poverty. [xxx] Many other Americans live just above the poverty level making it difficult for them to make ends meet let alone having any income left for savings, retirement, any medical bills, etc. Having a nice place to live or taking their family on vacation is impossible. Many of these individuals are not unemployed but are only able to find jobs that pay minimum wage; some of these individuals work two or more jobs to try and make ends meet and support their families. Most of us know these families and the struggles they face. Some of us may have even been in a similar position during our lives, barely making enough to support our families and hoping we can make it through each day without any major problems. For these individuals it only takes one issue, someone in their family has a major health issue, a car breaks down, rent goes up, etc., to drastically change their livelihood and the little stability they know.

At one time, unions helped many workers by negotiating fair wages, better working conditions, and benefit packages such as health insurance, retirement, and sick leave. However, many of the labour unions which protected workers no longer exist to protect workers. The demise of unions is partially attributed to greed. When unions were strong many of their leaders became corrupt and complacent, no longer in the best interest of the workers but using their power and influence to line their pockets.

With the decline of organized labour unions, many companies have cut employee benefits to reduce costs and increase profits. Within several decade's many companies have:

- Moved some of their functions out of the United States to countries with cheaper labour and less government labour laws to boost their profits.
- Reduced the number of full-time employees replacing their workforce with part-time employees thus cutting benefits normally provided to full-time workers.
- By stashing profits offshore thus avoiding paying U.S. taxes

During the Great Recession, many companies saw record profits while many Americans lost their jobs, their benefits, and their homes. Greed was a major factor in the Great Recession and continues to plague our country.

Greed is an evil that has always plagued the world. In a way we all are guilty of greed in some way; we all would love to have more than we need to live and survive. The difference is the majority of us work hard to earn what we have while others prey on us to benefit themselves.

We all see it, and it appears to have gotten worse over the years. Like most of us, I was taught that you should always take pride in what you do, work hard, if you can't afford something to do without, thank God for what you have, and don't take advantage of others. I also was taught we should help those in need and less fortunate and not judge anyone because we don't know what they may be going through in their lives. Both my parents worked hard starting at a very young age. My father who grew up during the Great Depression, worked with his brothers and sisters to help support their mother and the family. At 17 he joined the military and fought in WWII and the Korean War retiring in the late 1960s. After retiring from the military, he worked several jobs to support our family, working until he was able to retire at 62. My mother who grew up in Alsace, France during WWII never knew her father, who died two months before she was born. She helped her mother raise her brothers and sisters and continued to work until the age of 62. During the 1970s there were times when my father was laid off from his job, but like most people back then, he was too proud to accept any assistance. Instead, he would find odd jobs to support us. My mother would plant a garden and grow food to help feed the family, something we don't see much of in today's society.

Over the years, we have seen an increasing number of people requesting and receiving government assistance mostly out of necessity such as:

- Individuals who lost their jobs, also lost their health insurance, some also losing their homes have had to request assistance to survive.
- Those lucky to find work often had to accept jobs at a lower salary and with no benefits such as health insurance.
- Families or single parents who are unable to find a living wage and affordable health care

Most of these individuals require government assistance and will continue to request assistance until they can get back on their feet.

Then there are the other few individuals who are greedy and receive government assistance even though they could support themselves and don't necessarily need assistance. They are the individuals:

- who refuse to work and expect everyone else to support them

- who could find work but refuse to accept a position which they feel is beneath them
- whose entire purpose is to locate and abuse the system for anything they can get for free

These are the individuals who have no respect for themselves or anyone else or no pride. These are the individuals that give fodder to individuals who want to scrap government welfare programs altogether.

Medieval theologian Thomas Aquinas said this of Greed: *"it is a sin directly against one's neighbour, since one man cannot over-abound in external riches, without another man lacking them... it is a sin against God, just as all mortal sins, inasmuch as man contemns things eternal for the sake of temporal things."*

Priorities Not Consistent with Our Values as a Nation of Christians

The priorities of our country no longer reflect what our country was founded on and goes against our Christian values. As stated above our country are no longer leads the world in areas such as education, income equality, and trade. It appears the only areas the United States is ranked number one in are:

- Defense spending - to put into perspective, the U.S. government spends approximately $610 billion a year about 20% of all federal spending. The amount is more than what China, Russia, Saudi Arabia, France, United Kingdom, Germany and India combined spend on their defense.[xxxi]

- Incarcerations - the United States has the largest prison population in the world. According to the US Bureau of Justice Statistics (BJS), in 2013, 2,220,300 adults were incarcerated in US federal and state prisons, and county jails.[xxxii]

- State and local spending on incarceration has grown three times as much as spending on public education since 1980, according to a 2016 analysis of federal data by the U.S. Education Department.[xxxiii]

- Gun ownership – There are more than 300 million guns in the U.S., 112.6 for every 100 people, more guns than people.[xxxiv]

- And gun violence - The United States also has the highest homicide-by-firearm rate among the world's most developed nations.

Americans should find the above appalling and embarrassing. Having the highest defense spending and gun ownership reflects the number of resources special interests groups use to promote these items. Having the world's highest incarceration rate and gun violence can be associated somewhat with the income inequality in our country but also, as parents and society, the values we instil in our children.

We need a strong defense to protect our country, however, at what cost? Instead of continually increasing our defense budget our elected officials should look for ways of reducing the cost and size. As a country, we should be reducing the number of military installations we have around the world. The Department of defense should only keep bases which are strategically important to our defense and those of our allies. As a nation we can no longer afford to try and defend the world nor should we. We should never be aggressors but only use our military to defend ourselves against those who are hostile against us.

According to several reports, The Iraqi war cost American taxpayers over 2 trillion dollars[xxxv]. That is not including the thousands of American soldiers who lost their lives, the thousands who returned with severe injuries and disabilities, and the millions of Iraqi citizens who lost their lives. The lives and money spent on that needless war could have been used to establish a universal health care program, to offer free higher education to our citizens, rebuild our countries infrastructure and reduce our deficit.

The U.S. has the largest prison population in the world. Why? Are Americans more prone to commit crimes than any other country in the world? More needs to be done to reduce the prison population in our country. I believe a lot of the problems with crime involve the upbringing of an individual, the lack of education, greed and poverty. Unfortunately, many parents don't spend enough time with their children to teach them right from wrong, to respect others and themselves and basic values. As parents, we need to spend time with our children and teach them good values.

Numerous studies on the prison population show there is a correlation between poverty and education. Maybe if we reduced poverty in our country and improved our educational system crime would decrease. In any event, more needs to be done in to reduce crime in our country.

The U.S. has the highest gun ownership among its population in the world. There is nothing wrong with owning a gun; in fact, it is a Constitutional right.

*"A well regulated Militia, being necessary to the security of a free State, the **right** of the people to keep and bear Arms, shall not be infringed."* – U.S. Constitution 2nd Amendment.

However, there needs to be a control on the sales and ownership of guns in the U.S. to decrease the tens of thousands of death and injuries which occur annually.   Just like a driver's exam is required to operate a motor vehicle, anyone who wishes to own a gun should be required to complete a background investigation and gun safety course. There have been far too many deaths due to a few individuals who shouldn't have been able to purchase weapons and have been careless with weapons.

According to the National Crime Victimization Survey, in 2011, 467,321 persons were victims of a crime committed with a firearm[xxxvi]. In the same year, data collected by the FBI show that firearms were used in 68 per cent of murders, 41 per cent of robbery offences and 21 per cent of aggravated assaults nationwide.[xxxvii] Over the past several years we have seen an increase in shootings in schools.

- April 16, 2007, at Virginia Tech an individual killed 32 students, faculty and staff with a firearm
- On July 20, 2012, a shooter at the Century 16 movie theatre killed twelve people and injured 70 others.

- December 14, 2012, Newtown, Conn., Twenty-seven people, including 20 elementary school

children, were killed by a gunman who then shot and killed himself
- June 17, 2015, Charleston, S.C., A gunman opened fire and killed nine people during a prayer service at a historic African American church in downtown Charleston.
- October 1, 2015, Umpqua Community College in Roseburg, Ore., nine people were liked when bullets tore into classrooms.
-

The number of shootings killing innocent people goes on and on yet there continues to be nothing done to regulate or control guns in our country. Why? I believe the main reason is special interest groups such as the National Rifle Association and weapons manufacturers that have spent millions of dollars to convince the populace that any gun control would be the equivalent of taking everyone's guns away, which is far from the truth. No one wants to see their 2nd Amendment right to bear arms taken away but have requirements on gun ownership to reduce the number of unnecessary deaths from guns. It's a matter of common sense to have controls on dangerous items such as guns which contribute to most of the homicides in the U.S.

As Christians we are taught to treat others as we want to be treated, help the poor and those in need, respect and obey God's laws, don't steal or cheat others, and don't judge our fellow man. If we as a nation of Christians committed ourselves to abide by these teachings, there should be no question on what we as a nation need to accomplish.

We as Christians need to elect individuals who will get our country's priorities straight and back on track. We need to start by helping each other and those in need. We need to demand changes be made to our healthcare and education system so we can provide our citizens with affordable health care and our children with the education they need to be competitive in the world. We need to demand our government to spend our money wisely with a more effective and efficient system. And we need to condone and report those who try to manipulate and take advantage of our system for their benefit and greed.

We all need to work together as a nation and stop blaming one another when things go wrong and blaming a certain group of individuals for the problems which come up. Everyone should be on an equal plain. We shouldn't concern ourselves on what is politically correct but what is best for the entire country. If we can somehow manage this, we will be able to get our country back on the right track.

Getting back on Track

Since the establishment of our country, it has gone through many changes, good and bad. However, in the past couple of decades, our country has become more and more divided, not only politically and socially but economically. Our values and the foundation on what our country was founded seem all but forgotten. Individuals who are only concerned about themselves and what they can gain should not control our county; only individuals who want what is best for all citizens and the country.

There are many common sense ways of getting our country back on track. Initially, we need to improve the way we select and elect our officials. Individuals who run for public office should be transparent in who they are and what they stand for on issues. We as citizens should do our homework to have a clear understanding of the candidates. I believe candidates should only be able to receive limited contributions to their campaigns from citizens and not from special interest groups and companies. Each candidate should receive equal time to discuss their stand on specific topics and any advertisements for or against a candidate should be based on facts or not allowed. Of course, this will probably never happen, but it would hamper outsiders and special interest groups interfering with our elections.

I also believe all our citizens should be required to have a national identity card. A national identity card could serve several purposes:

- Ensure the individual is a U.S. citizen
- Used to confirm an individual's right to vote
- Used to obtain any government aid or benefits
- Be turned in to proper authorities when an individual is deceased
-

If the implementation of a national identity card is properly administered and required for the above it will assist in deterring voter fraud, unauthorized individuals obtaining government aid or benefits, identity theft and other potential forms of fraud.

Secondly, there needs to be a change in the way the government does business. Our government system is known for its wasteful spending which is partially due on the way the system is set up and run.

Presently, there are areas which both Republicans and Democrats seem to agree upon such as reducing the deficit and forming a more efficient and effective government. However, neither party can seem to agree or compromise on a solution to fix these areas. The Republicans want to reduce or eliminate social programs with no new taxes or tax hikes and the Democrats want to reduce the deficit by cuts in government programs such as defense and tax hikes on wealthy Americans.

It's no secret there has always been and continues to be tremendous fraud, waste, and abuse within the government. Despite numerous headlines and reports very little seems ever to get done to address and correct this problem. Politicians are very quick to acknowledge the problems especially when they make headlines yet do very little to try and find some solution to correct them. Instead, they use it as fodder to attack their opponents placing the blame on others. In other words all talk with very little action. The sad fact about it is if our elected officials would take the time to look into these issues and find ways to correct them they would save billions of taxpayer dollars. Money that could be used to rebuild our infrastructure, assist those in need and reduce taxes -issues representatives from both parties raise during fundraisers and speeches. So if everyone agrees on reducing or eliminating waste, fraud, and abuse, which they all claim to agree on, then why hasn't anything been done to correct or address these issues? Is it because they are intimidated by the size of the government? Maybe they don't know or can't agree on where to begin the process. Maybe they are afraid any changes may backfire on their chances for re-election. Maybe cuts or realignments within certain agencies may impact on their constituents. Maybe they are afraid it will hurt some private industries and favors they promised to some of their wealthy campaign donors. Or maybe they can't see spending their time and efforts to correct them. Whatever the reason or excuse nothing or very little seems to be getting accomplished in the area of waste, fraud, and abuse.

If Congress is serious about reducing fraud, waste, and abuse in the government there are several measures they should consider as well as numerous reports, from the Government Accountability Office (GAO), Project on Government Oversight (POGO) and other nonpartisan agencies which outline some of these issues and recommend viable changes. Congress also needs to change how government conducts business to make it more efficient and effective and provide the necessary oversight to ensure it is run properly.

Ways, the government, can be more efficient and effective

There are several ways to make a more efficient and effective government, but it will require support from Congress, the White House, and the voters. There are several ways the government can reduce costs and become more efficient and effective:
1. Reducing the number of contract employees.
2. Reducing overlap and duplication among agencies/departments
3. Change the mentality of how government agencies/departments do business
4. Standardize systems across the government

Reducing the size of the Federal Government
Most politicians often state the federal government is too big and should be smaller. However, there seem to be disagreements between Republicans and Democrats on how to accomplish this

task. Many politicians, especially Republicans, believe agencies such as the Internal Revenue Service, Housing and Urban Development (HUD), Environmental Protection Agency, Department of Education and agencies which support entitlement programs should be reduced or eliminated. Others, primarily Democrats, believe a reduction in the size of the government should be done by attrition and finding ways to making government agencies/departments more efficient. Unfortunately, talks by both parties in reducing the size of the government is just that talk. In fact, during George W Bush's administration, the size of the federal government grew not only in spending but also in the number of federal civil servants and a huge number of government-funded contractors.

The use of contract workers in the federal government seems to be a popular way for politicians to hide the true size of the government since no one within the government seems to track contractors. In fact, in 2015, Congressman Chris Van Hollen asked the Congressional Budget Office (CBO) for the number of contractors employed by the Federal government. On March 11, 2015, the Director of CBO responded in a letter stating there are no records which accurately show the number of contract employees who work for the federal government. The letter goes on to state that the Inventory for contract of services (ICS) reported that in 2012 129 billion dollars was spent on covered service contracts and that those contracts paid for 670,000 contractor positions at an average cost of about $193,000 per full-time contractor, more than 2.7 times the cost of the average federal civilian position. [xxxviii]

Anyone who works or has worked in the past few decades for the federal government would believe the number of contractors within the federal government is in the millions. According to OPM in 2011, there were 4,403,000 federal employees (2,820,000 civilian and 1,583,000 uniformed military personnel) within the federal government. In 2010, the annual cost for civilian was

150,321 million dollars. Also, there were approx — 8 million contract employees which cost taxpayers over 320 billion dollars a year. [xxxix]

I recall after the September 11 terrorist attacks the federal government began to hire thousands if not millions of contractors. The FBI hired a lot of contractors to work as language specialists and investigative assistants. In 2004, when I began to work for the Department of Defense the Command, where I was assigned, had more contractor employees than military and civilian personnel combined. Most of the contract workers were military reservists and military retirees working as contractors. It is a common practice among many federal workers that upon retirement they obtain a lucrative position as a contractor. Many, would retire on a Friday and return to work on the following Monday as a contractor, drawing their federal pension and making twice the money as a contractor that they made while a civilian or active duty military member. Not a bad post-retirement career.

What is interesting about the contract workforce is that initially when the government began hiring contract employees; it was supposed to be short term, hiring them to assist the civilian workforce in catching up on any backlogged work. However, as I found that was not the case. For many contract employees working for the federal government was not temporary but a career in itself with higher salaries and benefits than most federal career employees. In 2004, when I began working for the Department of Defense the Department where I worked employed five contract employees when I retired in 2017 the same five contract employees were still employed. One contract employee, a retired Army Lieutenant Colonel, was in charge of the other contract employees assigned within the department and was instrumental in bringing in other contractors into the department increasing the contract population within the department to over 20. Most of the contractors brought in were Army reservists of friends of the retired Lieutenant Colonel. Many did not have the experience required for the positions they were assigned which cost even more money for the government to train these contractors.

What many people don't understand is that not only do contractors cost the government more money for their services it also requires additional government resources to write the contracts, in some instances the government must pay for the contractor's background investigations and security clearances, and their training.

When one puts all the costs together hiring contractors instead of federal civil servants, do not make any sense and is a gross waste of taxpayers' money. By substantially reducing the number of contractors within the federal government and replacing them with civil servants the government would save billions of dollars a year.

Reducing the number of contract employees

According to OPM in 2011, there were 4,403,000 federal employees (2,820,000 civilian and 1,583,000 uniformed military personnel) within the federal government. In 2010, the annual cost for a government civilian was 150,321 million dollars. Also, there were **approx. Eight million contract employees cost** taxpayers over 320 billion dollars a year.[xl]

Anyone who has worked in the federal government in the past 20 years has seen a huge increase in the number of government contractors, especially after the September 11th attacks. This is partially due to continued demand for a smaller government, the reduction of civilian government employees gave the appearance government was shrinking in size even though the number of contractors who are not counted substantially increased. It is not unusual for a government worker to retire from federal service on a Friday and report back to work the following Monday as a contractor at higher pay. The government wastes billions of dollars a year using contract employees instead of hiring civilian employees. I recall after the September 11th attacks there was an influx of newly hired contractors. Government agencies such as the FBI stated that a backlog in work was partially to blame for not being able to uncover the terrorists responsible for the 9/11 attacks. Initially, the idea of hiring contractors was to assist the government in reducing some of the work backlogs which once completed the contract employees would no longer be needed. Under President George G. Bush the government doubled the number of contracts with industry. In 2007, the government paid corporations more than $400 billion to work for almost every government agency to include some of our most sensitive agencies such as the CIA. The majority of contract money went to companies that didn't have to compete for it or faced only limited competition. The government is paying most of the contract money to corporations to perform the kinds of services that normally federal employees would perform.

Eliminate Fragmentation, Overlap, and Duplication in the Federal Government

Over the past several years the Government Accountability Office (GAO) produced several reports to Congress identifying actions which would improve the efficiency and effectiveness of government. The reports provide a wealth of information and recommendations on reducing unnecessary programs. The reports identify billions of dollars in potential savings if Congress would spend time reviewing and acting on them. Unfortunately, some of the recommendations target politically popular causes and areas unpopular to some special interests groups reducing the chance Congress will ever act on them.

For example, the GAO's 2016 annual report identifies 92 new actions that Congress and the executive branch could take to improve the efficiency and effectiveness of government in 37 areas. GAO consider programs or activities to be fragmented when more than one federal agency (or more than one organization within an agency) is involved in the same broad area of national need, and there may be opportunities to improve how the government delivers these services, including the following examples:

- Department of Defense (DOD) Commercial Satellite Communication Procurements:
Enforcing existing acquisition policy and identifying opportunities to centralize DOD's procurement of commercial satellite communications (SATCOM) services could create opportunities to potentially save tens of millions of dollars annually. DOD depends on commercial SATCOM to support critical mission needs, from unmanned aerial vehicles and intelligence to voice and data services for military personnel. DOD spent over $1 billion leasing commercial SATCOM in the fiscal year 2012. Guidance from the Chairman of the Joint Chiefs of Staff requires the Defense Information Systems Agency (DISA) to procure all of DOD's commercial SATCOM. However, GAO found that the combatant commands and military services independently procured commercial SATCOM to meet their individual needs. For example, DOD reported that contrary to the Joint Chiefs' requirement approximately 34 per cent (about $290 million) of its fixed satellite commercial SATCOM services were procured outside of DISA in 2012. Utilizing a central point of contact could better position DOD to not only meet mission needs but also to maximize cost savings by consolidating commercial SATCOM purchases.[xli]

- Department of Homeland Security's (DHS) Human Resources Systems:
DHS's human resources administrative environment includes fragmented systems, duplicative and paper-based processes, and little uniformity in its data management practices. According to DHS, these issues compromise their ability to

effectively carry out its mission. In 2003, DHS initiated the Human Resources Information Technology (HRIT) investment to consolidate, integrate, and modernize the human resources information technology infrastructure of the department and its eight components. As part of the HRIT effort, DHS determined that it had 422 human resources systems and applications. GAO found in a February 2016 report that DHS had made only limited progress in implementing HRIT, in part due to a lack of involvement of the HRIT executive steering committee. Moreover, HRIT's strategy may not reflect DHS's current priorities, in part because the department had not updated the HRIT strategic planning document since 2011. In addition, we reported that DHS established the Performance and Learning Management System (PALMS) program to provide a system that will consolidate DHS's nine existing learning management systems into one system and enable comprehensive training reporting and analysis across the department, among other things. However, GAO found that selected PALMS capabilities had been deployed to headquarters and two components, but that full implementation at four components was not planned as of January 2016, leaving uncertainty about whether the PALMS system would be used enterprise-wide to accomplish these goals. Further, DHS did not fully implement effective acquisition management practices and therefore was limited in monitoring and overseeing the implementation of PALMS and ensuring that the department obtains a system that improves its learning management weaknesses, reduces duplication, and delivers within cost and schedule commitments. GAO made some recommendations to DHS to, among other things; address HRIT's poor progress and ineffective management. As of March 2016, GAO's recommendations have not been fully addressed.[xlii]

Fragmentation can also be a harbinger for overlap or duplication. Overlap occurs when multiple agencies or programs have similar goals, engage in similar activities or strategies to achieve them, or similar target beneficiaries. We found overlap among federal programs or initiatives in a variety of areas, including the following examples:

- Internal Revenue Service's (IRS) Public Referral Programs :

The IRS could potentially collect billions of dollars in tax underpayments through its nine public referral programs and save resources by better managing fragmentation and overlap, improving communication, and streamlining processes. Public referral programs enable individuals to submit information to IRS about tax noncompliance, and they are an important piece of IRS's overall enforcement strategy and can help reduce the net $385 billion tax gap—the difference between taxes owed and those ultimately collected. GAO reported in February 2016 that IRS does not have a formal mechanism to facilitate information sharing across all nine referral programs, which causes both the public and IRS to spend resources unnecessarily.

Additionally, the referral programs involve largely manual processes, which forces the IRS to spend resources reading and routing the referrals. In an October 2015 report, GAO also identified key problems specific to the whistleblower program that are discouraging whistleblowers from coming forward, which, in turn, limits the IRS's ability to close the tax gap. For example, few large awards have been paid, claims take years to process, and communication with whistleblowers is limited. Several recommendations to IRS, including that it establish a coordination mechanism to communicate across the multiple referral programs, develop an online referral submission process, streamline the review process, and improve external communication. IRS agreed with our recommendations and planned to implement the whistleblower recommendations by October 2016. IRS has not yet provided an action plan or time frames for other referral program recommendations as of March 2016. Until IRS takes these actions, it may be missing opportunities to assist the public, collect billions in uncollected taxes owed, and leverage resources to streamline processes, which could help it to better coordinate and identify possible efficiencies, as well as better manage fragmentation and overlap.[xliii]

- Financial Regulatory Structure:

The U.S. financial regulatory structure is complex, with responsibilities fragmented among multiple agencies with overlapping authorities (see fig. 2). As a result, regulatory processes are sometimes inefficient, regulators oversee similar types of institutions inconsistently, and consumers are afforded different levels of protection. In 2009, we established a framework for evaluating regulatory reform proposals and noted that an effective regulatory system would need to address structural shortcomings created by fragmentation and overlap. While changes made by the Dodd-Frank Wall Street Reform and Consumer Protection Act (Dodd-Frank Act) were consistent with some of the characteristics identified in this framework, the existing regulatory structure does not always ensure (1) efficient and effective oversight, (2) consistent financial oversight, and (3) consistent consumer and investor protections. As a result, the negative effects of fragmented and overlapping authorities persist throughout the system. For example, regulation of securities and derivatives markets by the Securities and Exchange Commission and the Commodity Futures Trading Commission, respectively, can create the potential for inefficiencies in the way markets are overseen because of differences in certain of the agencies' rules related to similar products.[xliv]

In a February 2016 report, we suggested that Congress consider whether additional changes to the financial regulatory structure are needed. Without congressional action, it is unlikely that remaining fragmentation and overlap in the U.S. financial regulatory system can be reduced or that more effective and efficient oversight of financial institutions can be achieved. In other aspects of our work, GAO found evidence of duplication or risk of duplication, which occurs when two or more agencies or programs are engaged in the same activities or provide the same services to the same beneficiaries, including the following example:

- Medicaid and Exchange Coordination:

GAO found that there is a risk of duplicative federal spending on health insurance coverage for individuals transitioning between Medicaid and federally subsidized health insurance purchased through the exchanges created under the Patient Protection and Affordable Care Act. If individuals have a change in income or are affected by other factors, their eligibility for Medicaid and subsidized exchange coverage may also change. As many low-income individuals experience income volatility, transitions between the two coverage types are likely. Federal regulations require that state Medicaid agencies and exchanges coordinate to facilitate these transitions, including transferring individuals' accounts to the appropriate form of coverage when eligibility changes occur. A limited amount of duplicate coverage may be expected and is permitted under federal law for individuals completing the transition from subsidised exchange to Medicaid coverage. However, GAO found in October 2015 that duplicate coverage was also occurring outside of this transitional period for example, in cases where individuals did not end their subsidized exchange coverage after being determined eligible for Medicaid. While the Centers for Medicare & Medicaid Services (CMS) within the Department of Health and Human Services (HHS) have taken some steps to minimize the potential for duplicate coverage in states with federally facilitated exchanges, we found that its policies and procedures were not sufficiently based on federal standards for internal control. GAO recommended that CMS establish a schedule for regular checks for duplicate coverage in states with federally facilitated exchanges and develop a plan to routinely monitor the effectiveness of the checks and other planned procedures to minimize duplicate coverage. HHS agreed and acknowledged steps it has taken and plans to take to minimize the risk of duplicate coverage. For example, HHS stated that its first check for duplicate coverage was underway in August 2015 and that it plans to analyze the rate of duplicate coverage identified. HHS also stated that it plans to monitor the rate of duplicate coverage identified in periodic checks and that it is working to implement additional internal controls to reduce duplicate coverage. As of March 2016, HHS was in the process of refining these checks, but had not completed another check or established a schedule for doing so, which could ultimately help protect the federal government from unnecessary and duplicative expenditures.[xlv]

GAO also identified actions in 25 areas for Congress or executive branch agencies to consider that could reduce the cost of government operations, better target resources, or enhance revenue collections for the Treasury, including the following examples:

- Disability Insurance Overpayments:

The Social Security Administration (SSA) may be losing billions of dollars through overpayments to beneficiaries of the Disability Insurance (DI) program and improper waivers of overpayment debt. In the fiscal year 2014, about 11 million individuals with disabilities and their dependents received approximately $143 billion in DI benefits, $1.3 billion of which SSA identified as overpayments. Additionally, SSA permanently waived over $2.4 billion in overpayment debt over the past ten years. In our October 2015 report, we found that SSA's process for handling work reports by beneficiaries has internal control and other weaknesses that increase the risk of overpayments, even when DI beneficiaries follow program rules and report work and earnings. Also, SSA's process for handling requests to waive overpayments lacks sufficient controls to help ensure appropriate decisions are made. GAO made several recommendations to improve SSA's handling of overpayments, work reports, and waivers, including that SSA study automated reporting options and improve oversight of work reports and waivers. SSA agreed with all of these except the recommendation to improve oversight of work reports. We clarified that oversight should help to ensure that staff are following proper procedures. As of March 2016, SSA has not fully addressed these recommendations. Until SSA takes these actions, it will likely continue to overpay beneficiaries and improperly waive overpayment debt, costing the federal government billions of dollars.[xlvi]

- Medicare:

In the fiscal year 2015, Medicare served about 55 million beneficiaries at a cost of $634 billion. GAO found that the program could save billions of dollars annually if Congress were to equalize the rates Medicare pays for certain health care services, which often vary depending on where the service is performed. For example, Medicare spending on hospital outpatient department services was over $40 billion in 2013 and is growing, in part because services that were typically performed in physician offices have shifted to more costly hospital settings. Following this shift, services once reimbursed at a lower total payment rate can be classified as hospital outpatient department services and reimbursed by Medicare at a higher rate, increasing program costs. We suggested in December 2015 that Congress equalize payment rates between physician offices and hospital outpatient departments for certain services. While the Bipartisan Budget Act of 2015 addresses this payment differential for some new providers, many providers will continue to be paid more than necessary for certain services, such as office visits.[xlvii]

- Defense Excess Property Disposal:

Federal civilian agencies could potentially achieve millions of dollars in cost savings if they were able to obtain more of DOD's available excess personal property through the disposal process rather than purchasing similar property through a private sector supplier. Each year the military services identify thousands of items of personal property including military equipment and material that they need to dispose of because the property is obsolete, not repairable, or excess to their requirements but still usable. Because this property was originally purchased with federal funds, the government seeks to promote its reuse by federal agencies to minimize new procurement costs. However, GAO found in a January 2016 report that DOD's process for disposing of excess personal property gives some nonfederal entities that participate in special programs such as state and local law enforcement agencies priority for excess property over some federal civilian agencies that may have similar needs.

Consequently, federal agencies are at risk of spending appropriated funds to acquire property that could potentially be obtained through DOD's disposal process at a lower cost. For the fiscal year 2014, DOD reported that excess and surplus personal property with a total original acquisition value of approximately $3.18 billion in nominal dollars was reutilized within DOD or provided to special programs, transferred to other federal agencies, or donated to eligible organizations such as state and local governments or nonprofit organizations. DOD recently revised its policies and procedures for disposing of excess personal property so that DOD components can obtain its excess property before special programs. Still, special programs could obtain such property before most federal civilian agencies and nonfederal entities. As a result, we recommended that DOD further reassess its property disposal process to determine whether additional changes are needed in the priorities given to recipients within the process. DOD agreed and stated that it plans to continue to review all aspects of the disposal process as part of its standard operating procedures. However, while we understand DOD already assesses its disposal process as part of normal operations, we maintain that DOD should separately assess the priorities in its disposal process to make more efficient use of federal funds.[xlviii]

- Medicaid:

GAO identified several opportunities to achieve cost savings within the Medicaid program, which in the fiscal year 2015 covered approximately 69 million beneficiaries at an estimated cost of $529 billion. For example, we found in February 2016 that CMS had not clarified or broadly communicated guidance regarding the appropriate methods for distributing supplemental payments to hospitals. Without such guidance, states may be shifting costs to the federal government by distributing payments that are counter to agency policy, including by making payments that are not commensurate with providers' provision of Medicaid services and that are based on the availability of provider and local government financing. GAO also found that CMS's oversight of Medicaid payments to institutional providers was limited, in part, by the lack of a policy and standard process for determining whether payments to individual providers are economical and efficient, as required by federal law. As a result, excessive payments states make to individual providers may not be identified or examined by CMS. For example, GAO found that some hospitals' total Medicaid payments exceeded the hospitals' total operating cost that is, the cost for all hospital services provided to all patients the hospital served. GAO made some recommendations related to Medicaid, and HHS concurred or partially concurred with all of them. Taking these actions should help CMS to achieve substantial cost savings and improve its oversight of the Medicaid program.[xlix]

- DOD Excess Ammunition.
DOD could potentially reduce its storage, demilitarization, and disposal costs by hundreds of thousands of dollars by transferring excess serviceable conventional ammunition, including small arms ammunition, to federal, state, and local government agencies. When a military service determines that serviceable ammunition is beyond its requirements that ammunition is offered to the other services. If that ammunition is not taken, it is transferred to the Army, which manages the stockpile of excess conventional ammunition and takes actions to demilitarize and dispose of it. In the fiscal year 2015, DOD spent about $118 million to demilitarize and dispose of conventional ammunition. We reported in July 2015 that DOD had reduced some of its demilitarization and disposal costs by transferring some excess ammunition to other government agencies, as opposed to demilitarizing and disposing of it, but that DOD does not have a systematic means for communicating with these agencies about available excess ammunition. Communicating systematically with other government agencies on available excess ammunition could help reduce the stockpile and save DOD in storage,

demilitarization, and disposal costs. We recommended that DOD develop a systematic means to make information available to other government agencies on excess ammunition, and DOD agreed with this recommendation. However, in conducting follow-up work in March 2016, GAO found that DOD continues to transfer ammunition to other government agencies on an informal basis and no formal process has been implemented. Without establishing a formal means to communicate with and provide other government agencies with information on available excess serviceable ammunition, DOD could miss opportunities to reduce its overall storage, demilitarization, and disposal costs.[1]

The above examples are just a few of several provided which if implemented would save millions of taxpayers' dollars. The Government Accountability Office provides several reports on areas of government waste and ways to I,improve government agencies and programs. Everyone should take the time to educate themselves with these reports to have a better understanding of how the government spend and wastes taxpayer money.

Government Waste

There has always been a tremendous waste in the U.S. Government. There have been rumours about the government spending $600 for a toilet seat and $500 for a coffee pot. Could that be possible? If you look at some budget items that Congress passed in their spending bills, it could be possible. The fact is the government wastes billions of dollars a year on items most find frivolous and crazy. There are several agencies, both private and public, that puts out a list every year of some of the obscure items included in our federal spending bills. For years Senator Tom Coburn, an Oklahoma Republican, put out an annual report on some of the ridiculous spending projects approved by Congress. Senator Coburn has since retired and Senator James Lankford, another Republican Senator from Oklahoma, has taken over and puts out an annual report titled "Federal Fumbles" which highlights some of the most egregious wasteful spending items passed by Congress. For example, Senator Lankford's 2015 Federal Fumbles report highlights some areas of wasteful spending, for example:

- A 43 million dollar gas station – The Department of Defense built a gas station in Afghanistan which cost taxpayers $42,718,739[li]
- A 2.6 million dollar program on weight loss for truck drivers -The National Institutes of Health spent $2,658,929 weight-loss program for truck drivers[lii]
- $250 million to train 60 Syrian rebels – Congress gave $500 million in federal tax money to train and provide equipment for at least 5,400 Syrian rebels fighting against ISIL. Over the next year, the Department of Defense (DOD) spent about half of that amount and managed to train an overwhelming force of 60 fighters. In other words, DOD spent about $4 million per rebel.[liii]
- $48,500 to study the history of tobacco use in Russia – National Institute of Health announced a $48,500 grant to produce a book entitled, Cigarettes and Soviets: The Culture of Tobacco Use in Modern Russia[liv]
- The Department of Defense spent $48 million in military supplies for Yemen that never made it out of a Virginia[lv]

The above are just a few examples but show how the government wastes billions of dollars of taxpayer's money. In 2017, the federal government spent close to 5 trillion dollars. If the government cut out the wasteful spending, had more oversight, reduced the number of contractors, and reduced the overlapping and duplication of many agencies, it could save billions of dollars a year. Money that could be used to provide a universal health care program for all Americans, provide free higher education or trades schools for our youth, and restore or ageing infrastructure.

Change the Way Government Does Business

Everyone seems to agree that there is a tremendous amount of waste in the government and there are some ways to reduce the amount of waste. The GAO provides comprehensive research and recommendations which would save billions of dollars if just a fraction of their recommendations are implemented. Cutting spending on wasteful or unnecessary programs/projects would save millions of dollars and substantially reducing the number of contract workers would save billions of dollars. However, the government could save more money if they simply changed the way they do business. Specifically,

- At the end of year money
- Empire building
- Give bonuses for being efficient and saving money – vs – rewarding leadership for wasteful spending

Each government agency/department is required to submit a budget to Congress every year to fund their organizations for the year. The budgets are based on a projection of what will be needed to operate each organization throughout the year. If necessary an agency/department can go back to Congress to request additional money above their budget submission if a need exists to fund a special program or function.

There is a mentality which has existed for years within the federal government that all budgeted money must be spent before the end of the fiscal budget year regardless of a need. The spending of the end of yeat money can be seen especially in September of each year when each agency/department rushes to spend money left over in their accounts. I have witnessed this in my over 32 years of government service. When operating the FBI's Counterintelligence Operations Training Unit at Quantico from 1995 –1998, FBI management would calculate money left over in the various accounts and tell us we needed to find ways to spend it before the end of September of each year. In September 1998, I was informed that there were over 2 million dollars that needed to be spent. With the money I was able to purchase 30 new vehicles, brand new radios, and over a years' worth of supplies for the FBI's surveillance training. Even with these purchases, there was still a lot of money left over which was given to another office to use at their discretion. In other words, no matter how much we tried to save money the money had to be spent at the end of the fiscal year to justify the need for continued funding. It was the same when working at the Defense Intelligence Agency. Before the end of the fiscal year, the remaining money was spent on unnecessary items; it was like Christmas in September. Even the remaining contract money was spent. The senior contractor, who was also a retired Army Lt. Colonel, would give the contractors additional hours, which would be billed to the government as overtime, to use up any leftover contract money, ensuring the money was spent even though there was no need for the additional work. This spending continues to be a common practice within the government.

Another area which is common in most, if not all, agencies/departments within the government is what I call "empire building". The mentality in the government is that if you want to move up in the government, you must figure out a way to build your empire. One way to move up in the federal government is to come up with a way to increase the size of an office. Promotions and pay raise in the government often depend not only on the position but if the position has supervisory responsibilities. So if you can convince leadership that you can provide some additional service(s) but require more resources which will require you to supervise more individuals you can move up. I witnessed this during my entire 32 years of federal civilian service.

For example, in 2004 when first reporting to USSTRATCOM the office consisted of approximately ten individuals,

- an Air Force Lt. Colonel,
- a Naval Criminal Investigative Service (NCIS) Special Agent,
- four GS 12 civilian analysts,

- and four contract employees.

By the time I retired the office had increased in size to over 50 individuals to include:

- a GS15 Division Head,
- an Air Force Lt. Colonel serving as an Assistant Branch Chief
- three branches each consisting of a GS 14 Branch Chief,
- an Army Major
- a GS13 Air Force Office of Special Investigations (AFOSI) Special Agent,
- Approximately 10 GS 13 Civilians
- And approximately 27 contract employees.

By increasing the size of the office from 10 to approximately 50 individuals, there was an additional need for supervisors and higher level positions within the office. To be fair, some of the additional responsibilities were justified but not to the extent the office needed to increase five times. In regards to the additional contractors, the majority of the contractors hired didn't have the knowledge or expertise to perform their duties. The government had to spend additional money to send them out to train them on the basic requirements needed to perform their jobs. What I found astonishing is that if a contractor left the senior contractor would try and quickly find another contractor to fill the vacancy, not because there was work that had to be done but to fill the seat so the contracting company could make money.

The government often uses the crisis du jour to justify increasing agency/department spending. After the September 11 terrorist attacks, Congress quickly provided additional funding to fight terrorism. This increase in funding assisted a lot of agencies, especially those within the Intelligence Community, Defense and law enforcement. All these agencies/departments saw a huge increase in their budgets to fight terrorism. Once the threat subsided somewhat the resources used to fight terrorism were placed in other areas such as in intelligence or counterintelligence.

The next crisis which made headlines was the insider threat problem. In 2010, a United States Army soldier, Bradley Edward Manning, disclosed nearly three-quarters of a million classified and sensitive documents through WikiLeaks. In 2013, Edward Snowden, a National Security Agency (NSA) contract employee obtained and leaked thousands of classified United States intelligence reports and information. These major disclosures of classified information prompted the government to enhance spending for the development of insider threat programs throughout the Intelligence Community. Every agency and department quickly began to start up Insider Threat programs. Just within the Department of Defense, insider threat programs were established or enhanced in not only in each service, Air Force, Army, Navy, Coast Guard and Marine Corps but also within each Command. Plus a new organization, the DoD Insider Threat Management and Analysis Center (DITMAC), was established which provided hundreds of new civilian and contract positions with little assistance in finding insider threats. It should be noted that there have always been insider threat programs within the government. The government's increased spending on these programs has enhanced the insider threat programs to a degree but has caused many agencies to go overboard by creating additional unnecessary entities with little oversight costing millions of taxpayer dollars.

Finally, if the government operated like most private companies, it could save billions of taxpayer money. The government does not operate for profit. However, that shouldn't discourage agencies/departments from being fiscally responsible. The government could save billions of dollars if it rewarded its managers for finding more efficient and effective ways to operate while still saving money. Agencies/Departments could save billions of dollars a year if the heads of these agencies/departments were rewarded by the money they save each year than trying to justify spending end of year money and pushing for budget increases each year.

Common Sense Solutions

If our country is to get back on track we as citizens need to demand our elected officials work together to find common sense solutions. The solutions need to be fair and reflect the values for which our great country was founded. We need to hold our elected officials accountable and demand they pass legislation which reflects what we the people want and not special interest groups.

Legislation and better oversight on:

- Reducing government waste
- Eliminating overlapping programs
- Changing the way the government does business
- Health costs and tort law are just a few areas our elected officials should address which will save billions of dollars a year.

Other very important issues which benefit all our citizens are the following:

- Universal health coverage - I believe most Americans want affordable health care for all Americans. Affordable health care is a very important part of life and is an essential part of reducing poverty in our country.
- Education. As a wealthy nation, we should invest more in educating our citizens. If we as a nation want to continue to have a competitive edge in the global economy we need to invest in our future. Unlike 50 years ago where a high school education was sufficient to obtain a living salary, today, individuals need to have at least a bachelor's degree or have a skill or trade to earn a living salary. The world is quickly changing and has become more competitive. Technology has rapidly progressed, and we need highly educated individuals to be competitive. We also need skilled labor to continue to build and update our dilapidating infrastructure. Providing free higher education

and trade schools to every citizen would allow them to obtain the skills needed to earn a living wage.

- Reforming welfare programs – welfare programs need to be reformed to ensure only those in need receive assistance. Of course, there would be less need for welfare if a universal health care program was implemented and every citizen was able to receive the education and skills needed to earn a living wage. No one capable of working and earning a living wage should receive welfare. It should be only for individuals who are unable to work or earn a living wage. Individuals who are not making a living wage should receive assistance until they can earn a living wage.

UNIVERSAL HEALTHCARE

The U.S. is the only developed country in the world without universal health care coverage.

The U.S. is the only country out of wealthy nations that do not have universal health coverage for its citizens. Healthcare coverage in the United States compared to other countries is ranked at the very bottom. The chart below shows the countries of the world that have universal health care. It was produced by the Organization for Economic Cooperation and Development, a group of 34 countries seeking to improve trade.

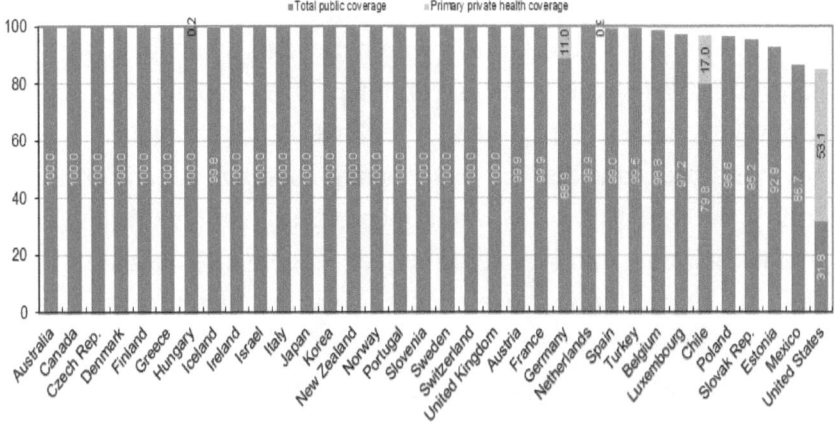

lvi

On March 23, 2010, President Obama and the Democrats passed the Affordable Care Act which was a start in assisting many Americans to access health insurance and helping individuals who were unable to obtain health insurance due to preexisting health conditions. Unfortunately, many of the insurance policies associated with the Affordable Care Act have extremely high deductibles and only cover very basic health coverage. Making it difficult for lower-income individuals and families to obtain the health coverage they need, it is a start in assisting many with some health care but still lacks in providing affordable health coverage to all Americans. Many Democrats lauded the Affordable Care Act as a positive move forward for all Americans while the Republicans reject the Affordable Care Act as being a form of socialism and too costly. In fact, since the Affordable Care Act was made into law Congressional Republicans have tried numerous times to repeal the law stating it is not good for America.

Healthcare for all Americans would be good for America. The biggest issue and challenge for obtaining affordable health care for all Americans is the cost and the stigma that universal health care is a social program. Individuals who believe in true capitalism vies universal health coverage as just another form of socialism. Far right groups have spent millions of dollars on ads to try and convince Americans that universal health coverage is bad for the country and that it hasn't worked in countries that have it such as Canada, England, and France. The fact of the matter is that it has been very successful in those countries and the citizens of those countries are happy with the care they have in place. Individuals in other countries find it hard to believe that the United States doesn't have adequate health care coverage for all its citizens. The below chart shows the overall views of citizens from 11 countries of their country's health care system:

Overall Views of Health Care System, 2013

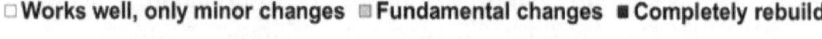
☐ Works well, only minor changes ☐ Fundamental changes ■ Completely rebuild

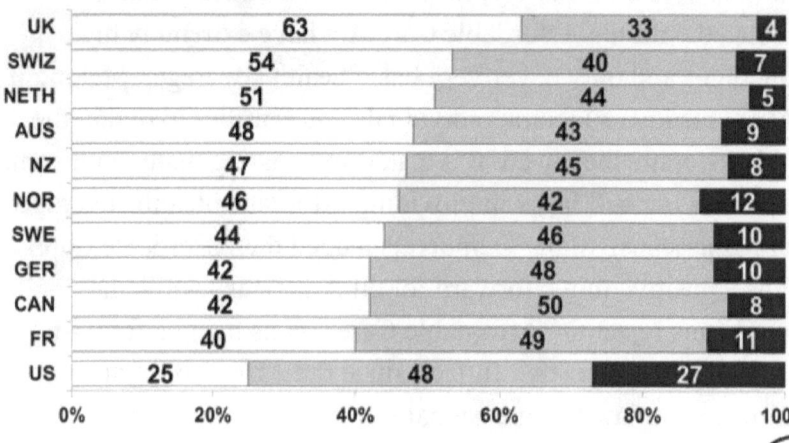

	Works well, only minor changes	Fundamental changes	Completely rebuild
UK	63	33	4
SWIZ	54	40	7
NETH	51	44	5
AUS	48	43	9
NZ	47	45	8
NOR	46	42	12
SWE	44	46	10
GER	42	48	10
CAN	42	50	8
FR	40	49	11
US	25	48	27

Percent

Source: 2013 Commonwealth Fund International Health Policy Survey in Eleven Countries.

THE COMMONWEALTH FUND

Only one in four Americans believe health care in the United States is adequate with the majority believing the health care system should be changed.

With 75% of Americans believing the health care system in the United States needs to be changed why hasn't it been changed? And why are politicians so hesitant in passing a universal health care system?

One of the biggest hurdles in changing our health care system is educating people on the issue. There are too many interest groups such as the current health industry, hospitals, doctors, insurance and pharmaceutical companies that will potentially lose money if the system radically changes. All these special interest groups spend millions of dollars a year supporting politicians who will not support any changes to the health care system. Also, many media outlets that rely on advertisements from these groups or who owned by wealthy individuals who despise any changes to our current system because they feel it will go against what they believe to be a purely capitalistic system, make sure the public only hears negative aspects of a universal health care system.

Cost of health care in the United States

According to a 2013, Public Broadcast Service (PBS) article on how the United States compares with other countries on health care, the US spends 17.6 per cent of GDP on health care, more than most countries.[lvii] The high cost does not reflect better care; in fact, the care is comparable to care in countries which costs are substantially lower. Below is a chart from the Organization for Economic Cooperation and Development (OECD) showing 2010 total health expenditures per capita, public and private. OECD is an international economic group comprised of 34 member nations.[lviii]

US spends two-and-a-half times the OECD average

Total health expenditure per capita, public and private, 2010 (or nearest year)

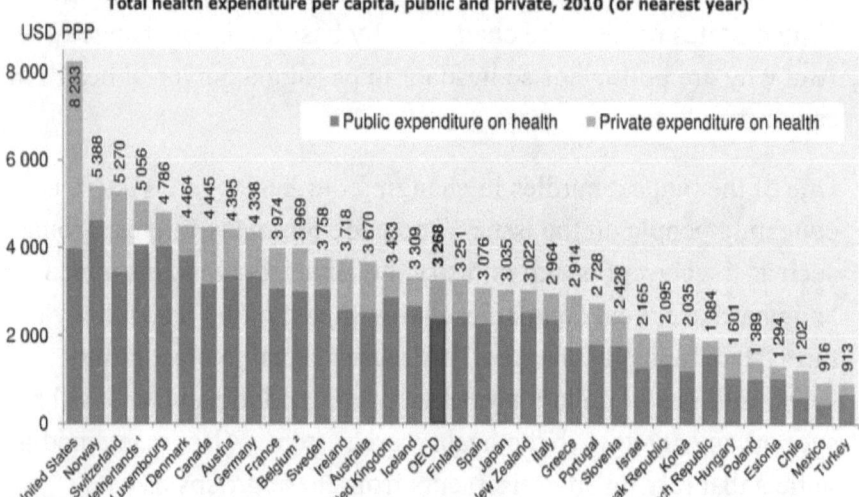

1. In the Netherlands, it is not possible to clearly distinguish the public and private share related to investments.
2. Total expenditure excluding investments.
Information on data for Israel: http://dx.doi.org/10.1787/888932315602.

Source: OECD Health Data 2012.

The high cost of care in the United States is due to some factors such as:

- Hospital costs – there is very little to no regulations as to what hospitals can charge for medical procedures. The average costs are 85% higher than in most other countries. Many countries have strong regulations which set prices hospitals can charge for services. It should be noted that the quality of care delivered in these countries' hospitals is comparable to that in the United States. [lix]

- High Malpractice Insurance – Doctors in the United States pay a very high malpractice insurance the cost of which is figured into what we pay.
- Unnecessary diagnostic procedures – Doctors in the United States tend to use additional tests, some of which are extremely expensive, to diagnose patients for fear of litigation.
- No set standards for procedure costs - Some hospitals and doctors will charge more to a patient depending on the patient's insurance. There are no set of standards in health care charges in many hospitals or doctors' offices.
- Prescriptions – In the United States many doctors overprescribe medications to their patients. Many pharmaceutical companies will pay hospitals and doctors to promote their new medications.

How to fix the health care problem in the United States

Health care is a complicated issue, especially when trying to provide good quality health care to every citizen. However, there are some things which can be done to reduce the cost.

- Establish specific guidelines outlining what hospitals and doctors can charge for specific procedures.
- Establish specific guidelines for malpractice to reduce frivolous cases.
- Establish regulations on the costs of prescription drugs
- Provide free education to individuals who wish to become doctors, nurses and medical technicians with the agreement they will work for a specific amount of years at a set pay schedule.

Of course, there is also the possibility of the government taking over health care and offering health care to all its citizens. Everyone pays a health care tax based on their income which would guarantee everyone has the same care and if done properly would save money. For example, we already pay taxes on Medicaid, Medicare, Veterans Administration (VA) health care and Tricare. Consolidating all these programs plus adding what most Americans currently spend on private health insurance and contribution some employers pay for their employee's health insurance into one department would easily pay for a universal health care program. Instead of seeing deductions in one's pay for private health insurance, and taxes for Medicare etc. there would only be one deduction for the universal health plan.

There are a lot of benefits in having a universal health care program.

- It would provide all Americans health care which would benefit everyone especially the poor.
- It would assist all employers. Employers would not have to offer health care benefits if there was universal health care saving them money.
- Everyone would have equal coverage
- If run properly universal health care would be more efficient. Processing claims would be consistent.

Passing any form of health care reform in the United States will be met with great resistance. Pharmaceutical companies, lawyers, hospitals, and doctors will all fight against any reforms or regulations which may impact their overall profit.

Education in the United States

Education is the foundation of improving our nation. It is one of the most important investments our country can make in keeping our county strong. A good educational system is essential in reducing poverty, boosting economic growth, and staying competitive with the rest of the world. It teaches us about the world around us and how to solve issues detrimental to our survival. However, the education system in our country is failing. Ranking of our education system has declined over the years, and we are no longer a world leader in education. It is imperative that we as a nation begin looking at our education system and find ways it can be improved. Our children and future depend on it.

- The World Economic Forum ranks the United States 52nd in the quality of mathematics and science education, and 5th (and declining) in overall global competitiveness
- The United States ranks 27th in developed nations in the proportion of college students receiving undergraduate degrees in science or engineering

We must provide a good educational foundation for our children as they grow through each phase of their educational life starting at the elementary level and continuing throughout college. Individuals who graduate from high school should be taught the essentials needed to survive in life. Many high school graduates are unable to do simple math such as figuring out the amount of change due in a transaction. We all witness or have been subjected to the above which appears more prevalent now than ten years ago. Just go to a store and pay your bill with cash, if the cashier is a young individual and the cash register doesn't calculate the change the cashier panics and makes an attempt to figure out the change. On many occasions, I have had to educate and assist the cashier in calculating the correct change.

Our country needs to improve our educational system to ensure all children have the opportunity to excel in life. After all children today will be our future leaders. We as a country should offer free education, not just through high school but college. Individuals who want to excel should be able to without having to worry about enormous student debt. Students should receive free tuition with the agreement that upon graduation the students repay their education by working as a public servant for the same amount of years they attended higher education. We could offer doctors free tuition if they agree to work in areas where a shortage of doctors exists.

In most European countries students learn basic skills up through high school. Students discuss their future goals with counsellors and before graduating high school are given a series of exams to determine if they are qualified to attend a university, attend a trade school or an apprentice program. Students who qualify for the university must pass to continue to the next year. If a student fails in a year, he/she can take that year over again. Students who fail two years in a row are disqualified from the program and must decide on a different lifetime goal. Education is free to all qualified students, and the university assists the students with a position upon graduation.

Public colleges and universities can also do their part in reducing the costs of what they pay for activities outside education such as sports. It is absurd for universities to spend millions of dollars on hiring a football coach instead of using the money to educate students. For example, Michigan paid over 9 million dollars for its football coach. We all love our sports and want our teams to win but at what cost? Taxpayers should have a say in what public schools pay coaches.

I realize that higher education may not be for everyone, individuals who are not inclined or who don't have the skills for higher education should have the opportunity to attend a trade school or internships in areas which may fit their goals. In many areas of our country high schools no longer offer courses in trades such as electrical, plumbing, auto mechanics, etc., causing a reduction of individuals with those skills. According to the Bureau of Labor Statistics, our country has a shortage of skilled workers with the demand for these workers increasing each year. The shortage of skilled workers will continue to be a huge problem within our country unless something is done to correct the problem.

Welfare

Welfare programs have always been a hot issue among many Americans since their inception. Many Americans believe there should be programs to help individuals in need, but many feel that individuals abuse these programs. Others believe it's not the responsibility of the government to assist those less fortunate. Some of our elected officials, mainly Republicans, have campaigned on a platform of reducing government assistance because they don't believe these programs are grossly abused and believe the government should not be in the business of handing out money to individuals or families in need. However, these same elected officials have no problem in providing taxpayer's money to support their cause(s). Most elected officials, mainly Republicans, in the Agricultural Belt are for cutting programs such as Medicaid, food stamps, and other entitlement programs but continue to support providing subsidies to farmers and corporations.

According to the U.S. Census Bureau, approximately 52.2 million (or 21.3 per cent) people in the U.S. participated in major means-tested government assistance programs each month in 2012. Participation rates were highest for Medicaid (15.3 per cent) and the Supplemental Nutrition Assistance Program, formerly known as the food stamp program (13.4 per cent).[ix] In FY2016, the U.S. government spent approximately $1,032 billion, including $591 billion in Medicaid, on welfare.

Participation in government assistance programs in an average month consisted of 41.6 per cent blacks, followed by Hispanics at 36.4 per cent, Asians or Pacific Islanders at 17.8 per cent, and non-Hispanic whites at 13.2 per cent.[lxi]

There has been some form of welfare since our country was established mainly for veterans; however, it wasn't until the early 1900s that our country began to initiate several programs to assist those in need. In the 1930s, the Great Depression which caused massive unemployment and economic turmoil made it necessary for the federal government to take action to assist the growing need of citizens who lost everything.

In 1935, the Social Security Act was passed and included direct relief to include food stamps and changes to unemployment insurance.

In 1964, under President Johnson's War on Poverty, the Economic Opportunity Act was passed. It was created "to eliminate the paradox of poverty amid plenty in this Nation by opening to everyone the opportunity for education and training, the opportunity to work, and the opportunity to live in decency and dignity."[lxii][lxiii] The Economic Opportunity Act also created the Office of Economic Opportunity which was responsible for administering most of the newly established programs such as Job Corps, Head Start, Legal Services and Community Action Programs. These programs assisted many by providing opportunities to learn a skill and be self-sufficient which lowered the poverty level in the United States at the time. Unfortunately, others saw these programs as a means to survive without having to work. These families are referred to welfare families, families that continued to depend on welfare programs for generations.

In 1996, under President William Clinton the "Personal Responsibility and Work Opportunity Reconciliation Act" was passed. The Act dramatically changes the welfare system by requiring work in exchange for time-limited assistance. The legislation was passed to end the so-called "welfare generation" by promoting the fundamental values of work, responsibility, and family and placing additional requirements on individuals on welfare. Americans left welfare rolls in droves after the passing of the legislation. Individuals receiving federal welfare payments fell to 6.3 million in 2000, about half the number of what it was before the passage of the Act.

Unfortunately, with the Great Recession of 2008 which caused an increase in unemployment and many people not only losing their jobs but also their homes and health insurance, welfare rolls once again increased. Since climbing out of the recession the unemployment rate has declined, however, a lot of individuals who lost their jobs during the great recession had to settle for lower-paying jobs, many also lost their homes and any safety nets they may have had. Many companies reduced if not eliminated employee benefits such as health insurance and retirement which has contributed too many families having to live in near poverty levels. These families continue to need government assistance such as food stamps and medical care to support their families.

There will always be a need for some form of welfare to assist those in need, especially with most businesses lowering or eliminating benefits such as health care and retirement. Individuals who are only able to find jobs that pay minimum wage are barely able to afford to take care of their families, let alone pay for high health insurance premiums, save money for their children's education or retirement. However, welfare should be only for those in need and should not be a continued form of livelihood. That said, there needs to be some accountability and oversight.

There needs to be a better system for distributing payments to those in need to ensure only those in need to receive payments. Several people who work in state agencies which approve and distribute these funds have told me that they were often forced to approve individuals to ensure all money received from the federal and state taxes were dispensed. The individuals receiving the assistance didn't meet the requirements and should not have received any assistance, but received it using all the funds. Then there are the few individuals who refuse to work and expect the government to support them and their family and individuals who abuse the system. These are the few individuals who ruin these programs for the truly needy.

Welfare programs should be administered at the lowest levels of government where it is easy to determine who needs them and who is abusing them. These programs should also be short term. The administrators of these programs should be assisting individuals in finding ways of getting them off welfare by assisting them in finding jobs, offering them training, etc. to assist them in becoming self-sufficient. I have found most individuals who receive some assistance would rather be self-sufficient and not have to rely on the assistance if at all possible. As taxpayers, we should demand our elected officials to find ways of improving the system to ensure it not only helps the truly needy but assists them in getting them off and not relying on welfare.

Defense Spending – we need to continue to have a strong defense. However, we spend more on defense than the top ten world military budgets combined. We need to rethink and prioritize our defense involvement in the world. Our defense should be used to defend our country and our allies when necessary. We should not enter into wars unnecessarily such as we did in the Iraqi war, but only when there is an imminent danger to our country and people. We should also consider reducing the number of military installations and troops around the world leaving only installations and troops in areas of strategic importance.

Gun Control – Gun ownership is a right given to us in our Constitution and therefore should be a right of all responsible citizens. There must be a common sense approach to gun ownership to ensure they are handled and stored properly. I believe anyone who wants to own a gun should be required to pass a background investigation and a gun safety course before being allowed to own a gun.

Tax Reform - All of us pay taxes, some more than others, and most of us don't mind paying taxes if the system was fair and the money spent is on items which help the country and our citizens. Our legislators need to work on reforming our present tax system to make it fair to everyone. Some individuals believe a flat tax for everyone would be the best way to reform our tax system. Whatever reform is implemented, any new tax system should be simplistic, fair, transparent, limit deductions and be fair to all.

World affairs – We as a nation should respect other countries cultures and way of life. We should not get involved in other countries affairs and spend more efforts on fixing the problems in our country. The U.S. spends billions a year on foreign aid. In 2014, the U.S. spent approximately 35 billion dollars on foreign aid, money which could have been used to help our citizens. Most Americans would be appalled if they knew how much of their tax dollars are used to provide military aid, health care and food to other countries. Money which could be used for our citizens.

Many of our citizens are oblivious on how our government spends our tax dollars. Billions of dollars are wasted or used on programs which don't necessarily are good for Americans. We as taxpayers need to demand transparency and hold our elected officials accountable on the spending of tax money. It just makes common sense.

Conclusion

"We the People of the United States, in Order to form a more perfect Union, establish Justice, insure domestic Tranquility, provide for the common defense, promote the general Welfare, and secure the Blessings of Liberty to ourselves and our Posterity, do ordain and establish this Constitution for the United States of America."[lxiv]

The Preamble of our Constitution sums up why our founding fathers wrote the document and its purpose. It affirms that we the people of the United States, not special interest groups, are in charge of our country and its destiny. As citizens, we need to get more involved in our political system and not allow special interest groups or greed steer the future path of our great country. As citizens, we should elect government officials who will do what is best for the country, sponsor common sense legislation which benefits the country and people, not special interests.

Many Americans don't take the time to review or get to know the candidates they vote for but vote their party line. Some individuals vote for candidates based on commercial advertisements, even though many of the television ads are paid for by special interest groups and not correct. As citizens, we all need to take the time to research candidates and make our selection based on who would be the best for the country.

There is a tremendous division within our country, a division not based on race or religion but financial inequality which is due, in some part, from legislation enacted by our elected officials. Among Americans, there are several different views, some extreme, on why our country has become so divided, but the bottom line is working-class Americans are finding it harder to make a living wage while the rich become richer.

Most Republicans believe in capitalism, and laissez-faire economics, less government control and regulations, more free enterprise, and less government spending on social programs is how the country should be run. A good concept if there were no greed. History has taught us that this ideology does not work. In the 19th century, when companies were allowed to operate with very little government regulations or control, we found there was a greater disparity in the distribution of wealth, a disregard for safety and the environment, and workers who were treated harshly often having to work 80 hours a week to survive. The government has to intervene to maintain a balance, protect consumers, workers, the environment, and the country.

History has also taught us that trickle-down economics doesn't work. The concept of reducing regulations and taxes for business will spur economic growth and profits which in turn business will use to pay employees better wages and benefits is a good concept except for greed. Instead of trickling down profits to workers businesses kept the profits.

On the other hand, most Democrats tend to go the other extreme. They believe there needs to be more government control and regulations to protect individuals, the environment, and the country. They believe the government should spend money on programs to help the poor, promote the arts, social justice, and affirmative action. This concept is also good except some aspects are extreme. History has taught us overregulation, and control deters growth and the more you give to help some the more they expect.

Everyone should have to pull their weight and be treated fairly; the government should not be responsible for supporting individuals who are simply lazy. There has to be an incentive to work. Why work if you don't have to especially when someone else pays your way and if you work you lose that assistance.

There has to be a better a more common sense approach to how we as a nation deal with the problems our society and people face. We should start by looking at areas in which we all agree needs fixed – more efficient and effective government, a balanced budget and less spending and start from there. We are all aware our government is very inefficient and wasteful so why not spend our efforts on finding ways to revamp our system to make it more efficient and effective. For example:

- Change the way government agencies operate by giving incentives to individuals who can make their agencies and departments efficient and effective and save money. Stop rewarding government agencies on what they spend by allowing them to return unused end of year money to the treasury and not penalizing them for not spending money not needed.
- Reduce overlap among the different agencies
- Reduce the number of contract employees
- Have better oversight on all programs

The government can save billions of dollars a year just by making the above changes which are a start. Next, we need to stop catering to special interest groups. Our elected officials need to promote legislation which is beneficial to our country and citizens and not special interest.

The Great Recession which occurred during the end of President George W. Bush's final term in office was partially due to a lack of government regulations and oversight on the financial markets. Both Republicans and Democrats are responsible for not seeing and fixing the problem before it was too late. Both parties were aware of what was happening but didn't do anything because they didn't want to upset special interests groups. The Great Recession not only cost many Americans their jobs and financial security but also trillions of dollars in taxpayer money. It's somewhat ironic that Republicans who believe the government should not be involved in regulating businesses or government spending approved stimulus packages to help failing businesses. Individuals who lost their jobs went on unemployment and received unemployment benefits, some also needed additional assistance in the form of food stamps, Medicaid and housing allowances from the government, costing the government even more money. The unemployment rate in the U.S during this time was close to 10%, and many of those unemployed also lost their health insurance and home, causing the poverty level to increase.

President Obama was able to get our country back on track, and the recovery spurred economic growth thus lowering the unemployment rate. Many of the individuals who lost their jobs during the Recession were able to find other positions; however, at a substantially lower salary and benefits.

To prevent another collapse of the financial institutions, President Obama enacted policies such as the Dodd-Frank Wall Street Reform and Consumer Protection Act, which gave the government more oversight of the financial institutions and a means of protecting American consumers. He also enacted the Patient Protection and Affordable Care Act which gave millions of Americans access to health coverage. The Act was not the best system but provided millions of Americans with some health insurance coverage.

Many Republicans saw the passage of the Affordable Care Act as a form of socialism and another welfare program costing taxpayers millions of dollars a year. The fact of the matter is that although flawed it provided relief to millions of Americans. Republicans and special interests groups continue to fight to have the Act repealed which would leave millions of Americans without any form of health coverage.

The U.S. needs to stop getting involved in other countries affairs and should not attack another nation unless they provoke an attack. Our country has a surplus at the end of President William Clinton's term. It wasn't until George W. Bush was president that our country started accumulating a deficit. The deficit can be attributed partially to the September 11th attacks on our great nation which required a need for increased security to deter the possibility of additional attacks. It also can be attributed to the war in Afghanistan and the Iraqi War.

Both of these wars cost thousands of American lives and approximately 2.4 trillion dollars. The war in Afghanistan can be justified by its correlation with the September 11th terrorist attacks. However, there is no real justification for the U.S. attacking Iraq. The war in Iraq served no real purpose to the U.S. except for causing chaos in the Middle East and more resentment toward the U.S. The U.S is still spending millions of dollars on rebuilding the infrastructure in Iraq and Afghanistan, money we should be using to rebuild our infrastructure.

Our country spends more on defense than the total spent by the ten largest military budgets in the world. If we as a country stopped intervening in other countries affairs, we could dramatically reduce our defense spending. The money saved could be used to help rebuild our country's infrastructure and our poor.

It's a matter of setting our priorities to that of which reflects our needs as a country and our Christian beliefs.

Throughout its history, our country has faced numerous challenges, and we as a nation were able to come together and overcome them. Our country is faced with new challenges which will require all of us to stand together and tackle, not just for us but our children and the future of our country.

Billions of dollars can be saved by understanding how our government operates, making sound decisions and taking back control of our government.

As Americans, we all need to work together to make our country strong. We need to break down the walls between us and work as one. After all, we are all God's children; the dream of a better future for our children. It doesn't matter what our race, religion, sex, or ethnicity we are all the same and share the same goal, to be able to live a good life, have a decent job, be able to retire and see our children succeed. We need to stop blaming each other for the problems we face and work together to resolve them.

No one should receive preference because of their ethnicity, race or sex but treated equally. Showing preference for one group of individuals only causes resentment. We need to provide our children with a good base to start their lives and future.

No one should have to worry about what they will do after graduating high school. We need to offer our children the opportunity to continue onto college or a trade school so they can start a career with a living wage. We also need a Universal health care system so families won't have to worry about receiving medical when needed and how they are going to afford it. These two items are critical to providing a good foundation for everyone.

As a country, we need to help those who are in need. However, we should keep in mind that no one, especially the government, owes anyone a living. The government should be there to protect us and assist when needed, but this should only be short term until an individual can get back on their feet.

I'm writing this book for several reasons:

1. I don't believe most Americans have any idea of how much fraud, waste, and abuse exists within the government. If we educate ourselves and work together, we can change the amount of fraud, waste and abuse in the government.

2. The influence special interest groups have on our system, most of which are interested in their welfare and not that of our country.

3. Our country is extremely divided, and we need to work together to bring it back together. We need to stop blaming each other for the problems in our country. Our problems are not due to our color, sex or ethnicity. We don't need to find ways to separate us more but unite us.

4. Our country needs to get its priorities straight if we want to continue to be competitive in the world.

5. Our politicians need to focus on what is best for the country.

I hope this book will provide some information which will spur debate and hopefully make some changes. I realize that change will be slow and painful but if made will help our country and citizens.

I also hope we all will work together to demand change and work toward the goal of making the country good for all and not just a few.

God Bless America!!

ABOUT THE AUTHOR

John Cole served in the Federal government for 32 years, 13 years with Defense Intelligence Agency as a counterintelligence agent and 19 years with the Federal Bureau of Investigation as a counterintelligence program manager, until his retirement in 2017.

He was born in France and moved to the U.S when he was an infant. He grew up in Plattsmouth, Ne, a small rural town outside of Omaha. He attended Plattsmouth High school graduating in his junior year. After high school, he joined the U.S. Air Force. After a short tour in the Air Force, he spent four years attending the Universite de Strasbourg, France where he studied the culture, political system, language and history of France. He returned to the United States and began working for the FBI and DIA.

---

[i] Fligstein, N. & Goldstein, A. (2014). The transformation of mortgage finance and the industrial roots of the mortgage meltdown.

[ii] Fligstein, N. & Goldstein, A. (2014). The transformation of mortgage finance and the industrial roots of the mortgage meltdown.

[iii] Fligstein, N. & Goldstein, A. (2014). The transformation of mortgage finance and the industrial roots of the mortgage meltdown.

[iv] Fligstein, N. & Goldstein, A. (2014). The transformation of mortgage finance and the industrial roots of the mortgage meltdown.

[v] Fligstein, N. & Goldstein, A. (2014). The transformation of mortgage finance and the industrial roots of the mortgage meltdown.

[vi] FactCheck, Obama's final numbers, September 28, 2017, Brooks Jackson

[vii] FactCheck, Obama's final numbers, September 28, 2017, Brooks Jackson

[viii] FactCheck, Obama's final numbers, September 28, 2017, Brooks Jackson

[ix] FactCheck, Obama's final numbers, September 28, 2017, Brooks Jackson

[x] FactCheck, Obama's final numbers, September 28, 2017, Brooks Jackson

[xi] CNNbusiness, US deficit rises 17% to highest level since 2012, October 16, 2018, By Lydia DePillis. https://www.cnn.com/2018/10/15/economy/us-budget-deficit/index.html

[xii] https://www.washingtonpost.com/politics/2019/01/21/president-trump-made-false-or-misleading-claims-his-first-two-years/?utm_term=.aadbc6d3c6bc Washington Post article dated 1/21/2019 by Glenn Kessler, Salvador Rizzo and Meg Kelly titled President Trump made 8158 False or misleading claims in his first two years.

[xiii] United Nations Human Rights Council report titled " Report of the Special Rapporteur on extreme poverty and human rights on his mssion to the United States of America" dated 4 May 2018 A/HRC/38/33/Add.1

[xiv] United Nations Human Rights Council report titled " Report of the Special Rapporteur on extreme poverty and human rights on his mssion to the United States of America" dated 4 May 2018 A/HRC/38/33/Add.1

[xv] United Nations Human Rights Council report titled " Report of the Special Rapporteur on extreme poverty and human rights on his mssion to the United States of America" dated 4 May 2018 A/HRC/38/33/Add.1

[xvi] United Nations Human Rights Council report titled " Report of the Special Rapporteur on extreme poverty and human rights on his mssion to the United States of America" dated 4 May 2018 A/HRC/38/33/Add.1

[xvii] United Nations Human Rights Council report titled " Report of the Special Rapporteur on extreme poverty and human rights on his mssion to the United States of America" dated 4 May 2018 A/HRC/38/33/Add.1

[xviii] http://www.census.gov/newsroom/press-releases/2015/cb15-157.html. United States Census Bureau, Income, Poverty and Health Insurance Coverage in the United States: 2014, dated September 16, 2015, Release Number: CB15-157

[xix] http://www.epi.org/publication/ib339-us-poverty-higher-safety-net-weaker Economic Policy Institute, U.S. poverty rates higher, safety net weaker than in peer countries, By Elise Gould and Hilary Wething | July 24, 2012 , Issue Brief #339

[xx] http://www.unicef-irc.org/publications/pdf/rc11_eng.pdf UNICEF Office of Research Innocenti Report Card 11 Child well-being in rich countries A comparative overview

[xxi] http://www.usnews.com/news/blogs/data-mine/2014/08/21/census-bureau-the-rich-got-richer-between-2000-and-2011 USNews, Census Bureau: The Rich Got Richer, By Katherine Peralta Aug. 21, 2014

[xxii] http://www.forbes.com/sites/frederickallen/2012/10/02/how-income-inequality-is-damaging-the-u-s/#23a34de430a2 How Income Inequality Is Damaging the U.S., Forbes, October 2, 2012,

[xxiii] http://www.nefe.org/press-room/news/the-benefits-blues.aspx
National Endowment for Financial Education, The Benefits Blues: A Growing Epidemic Among U.S. Workers, August 29, 2012, By Paul Golden

[xxiv] President George Washington's Farwell address 1796
https://www.ourdocuments.gov/doc.php?doc=15
[xxv] John Adams to Zabdiel Adams, 21 June 1776
https://founders.archives.gov/documents/Adams/04-02-02-0011

[xxvi] *Mian, Atif and, Sufi, Amir (2014). House of Debt. University of Chicago. ISBN 978-0-226-08194-6*
[xxvii] *Sowell, Thomas (2009). The Housing Boom and Bust. Basic Books. pp. 57–58. ISBN 978-0-465-01880-2*

[xxviii] Foreclosures up 75% in 2007, Defaults are way up for the year, with once red-hot Sun-Belt markets reporting the worst losses.
By Les Christie, CNNMoney.com staff writer, January 29 2008
http://money.cnn.com/2008/01/29/real_estate/foreclosure_filings_2007/

[xxix] Foreclosures up a record 81% in 2008 Filings continued to soar through the end of the year - and there's no relief in sight for 2009.
By Les Christie, CNNMoney.com staff writer, January 15, 2009
http://money.cnn.com/2009/01/15/real_estate/millions_in_foreclosure/

[xxx] U.S. Census Bureau, Income and Poverty in the United States: 2015. Report Number: P60-256, dated September 13, 2016 by Bernadette D. Proctor, Jessica L. Semega, Melissa A. Kollar

[xxxi] Peter G. Peterson Foundation, U.S. Defense Spending Compared to Other Countries, May 3, 2017, http://www.pgpf.org/Chart-Archive/0053_defense-comparison
[xxxii] Correctional Populations in the United States, 2013 (NCJ 248479). Published December 2014 by U.S. Bureau of Justice Statistics (BJS). Lauren E. Glaze and Danielle Kaeble, BJS statisticians.
[xxxiii] Emma Brown and Danielle Douglas-Gabriel (July 7, 2016). Since 1980, spending on prisons has grown three times as much as spending on public education. *The Washington Post.* Retrieved July 12, 2016.
[xxxiv] *Ingraham, Christopher (2015-10-05).* "There are now more guns than people in the United States". *The Washington Post.* ISSN 0190-8286. *Retrieved 2015-10-05.*

[xxxv] Iraq war costs U.S. more than $2 trillion: study, Reuters, March 14, 2013, by Daniel Trotta
http://www.reuters.com/article/us-iraq-war-anniversary-idUSBRE92D0PG20130314

[xxxvi] Bureau of Justice Statistics, *Nonfatal Firearm Violence, 1993-2011*, special tabulation from the Bureau of Justice Statistics' National Crime Victimization Survey, provided to NIJ January 2013.
[xxxvii] Federal Bureau of Investigation, "Crime in the United States, 2011."
[xxxviii] Letter to Congressman Chris Van Hollen from Director Congressional Budget Office, March 11, 2015. http://www.pgpf.org/Chart-Archive/0053_defense-comparison

[xxxix] United States Census Bureau, Federal Government Finances, Federal Civilian Employment,

2010 annual report.

xl United States Census Bureau, Federal Government Finances, Federal Civilian Employment, 2010 annual report

xli Government Accountability Office 2016 Annual Report: Additional Opportunities to Reduce Fragmentation, Overlap, and Duplication and Achieve Other Financial Benefits, April 2016, GAO-16-375SP

xlii Government Accountability Office 2016 Annual Report: Additional Opportunities to Reduce Fragmentation, Overlap, and Duplication and Achieve Other Financial Benefits, April 2016, GAO-16-375SP

xliii Government Accountability Office 2016 Annual Report: Additional Opportunities to Reduce Fragmentation, Overlap, and Duplication and Achieve Other Financial Benefits, April 2016, GAO-16-375SP

xliv Government Accountability Office 2016 Annual Report: Additional Opportunities to Reduce Fragmentation, Overlap, and Duplication and Achieve Other Financial Benefits, April 2016, GAO-16-375SP

xlv Government Accountability Office 2016 Annual Report: Additional Opportunities to Reduce Fragmentation, Overlap, and Duplication and Achieve Other Financial Benefits, April 2016, GAO-16-375SP

xlvi Government Accountability Office 2016 Annual Report: Additional Opportunities to Reduce Fragmentation, Overlap, and Duplication and Achieve Other Financial Benefits, April 2016, GAO-16-375SP

xlvii Government Accountability Office 2016 Annual Report: Additional Opportunities to Reduce Fragmentation, Overlap, and Duplication and Achieve Other Financial Benefits, April 2016, GAO-16-375SP

xlviii Government Accountability Office 2016 Annual Report: Additional Opportunities to Reduce Fragmentation, Overlap, and Duplication and Achieve Other Financial Benefits, April 2016, GAO-16-375SP

xlix Government Accountability Office 2016 Annual Report: Additional Opportunities to Reduce Fragmentation, Overlap, and Duplication and Achieve Other Financial Benefits, April 2016, GAO-16-375SP

l Government Accountability Office 2016 Annual Report: Additional Opportunities to Reduce Fragmentation, Overlap, and Duplication and Achieve Other Financial Benefits, April 2016, GAO-16-375SP

li Federal Fumbles 100 ways the Government Dropped the Ball, by US Senator James Lankford, 2015 https://www.lankford.senate.gov/imo/media/doc/Federal_Fumbles_2015.pdf

lii Federal Fumbles 100 ways the Government Dropped the Ball, by US Senator James Lankford, 2015 https://www.lankford.senate.gov/imo/media/doc/Federal_Fumbles_2015.pdf

liii Federal Fumbles 100 ways the Government Dropped the Ball, by US Senator James Lankford, 2015 https://www.lankford.senate.gov/imo/media/doc/Federal_Fumbles_2015.pdf

liv Federal Fumbles 100 ways the Government Dropped the Ball, by US Senator James Lankford, 2015 https://www.lankford.senate.gov/imo/media/doc/Federal_Fumbles_2015.pdf

lv Federal Fumbles 100 ways the Government Dropped the Ball, by US Senator James Lankford, 2015 https://www.lankford.senate.gov/imo/media/doc/Federal_Fumbles_2015.pdf

lvi http://www.oecd-ilibrary.org/sites/soc_glance-2014-en/06/05/g6-10.html?contentType=%2fns%2fChapter%2c%2fns%2fStatisticalPublication&itemId=%2fcontent%2fchapter%2fsoc_glance-2014-26-en&mimeType=text%2fhtml&containerItemId=%2fcontent%2fserial%2f19991290&accessItemIds=&option6=imprint&value6=http%3a%2f%2foecd.metastore.ingenta.com%2fcontent%2fimprint%2foecd&_csp_=ca32dec38ec6da78629969a1da242cf8

lvii Health Costs: How the U.S. Compares With Other Countries, BY Jason Kane *October 22, 2012, PBS http://www.pbs.org/newshour/rundown/health-costs-how-the-us-compares-with-other-countries/*

lviii Health Costs: How the U.S. Compares With Other Countries, BY Jason Kane *October 22, 2012,*

PBS http://www.pbs.org/newshour/rundown/health-costs-how-the-us-compares-with-other-countries/

lix Health Costs: How the U.S. Compares With Other Countries, BY Jason Kane *October 22, 2012, PBS http://www.pbs.org/newshour/rundown/health-costs-how-the-us-compares-with-other-countries/*
lx United States Census Bureau report titled "21.3 Percent of U.S. Population Participates in Government Assistance Programs Each Month", May 28, 2015, Release Number: CB15-97 https://www.census.gov/newsroom/press-releases/2015/cb15-97.html

lxi United States Census Bureau report titled "21.3 Percent of U.S. Population Participates in Government Assistance Programs Each Month", May 28, 2015, Release Number: CB15-97
lxii *Pollak, Stephen J.* "Major Acts of Congress | Economic Opportunity Act of 1964", *Economic Opportunity Act of 1964. eNotes. Retrieved 28 March 2011.*

lxiii *United States Statutes at Large*, volume 78. Washington D.C.: United States Government Printing Office, 1965. 508-516. Public Law 88-452, The Economic Opportunity Act, 1964 Public Law 88-452

lxiv The Constitution of the United States, Preample, National Archives, founding docs, constitution. https://www.archives.gov/founding-docs/constitution-transcript

www.ingramcontent.com/pod-product-compliance
Lightning Source LLC
Chambersburg PA
CBHW051357280526
45784CB00007B/2996